The
World's Greatest
Peanut Butter
Cookbook

THE
WORLD'S GREATEST
Peanut Butter
COOKBOOK

LINDA ROMANELLI LEAHY

WITH JACK MAGUIRE

VILLARD BOOKS · NEW YORK · 1994

Copyright © 1994 by Linda Romanelli Leahy and Jack Maguire

All rights reserved under International and Pan-American Copyright Conventions.
Published in the United States by Villard Books, a division of Random House, Inc.,
New York, and simultaneously in Canada by Random House of Canada Limited, Toronto.
Villard Books is a registered trademark of Random House, Inc.

Library of Congress Cataloging-in-Publication Data

Leahy, Linda Romanelli.
The world's greatest peanut butter cookbook/Linda Leahy with
Jack Maguire.—1st ed.
p.   cm.
ISBN   0-679-74659-5
1. Cookery (Peanut butter)   I. Maguire, Jack.   II. Title.
TX814.5.P38L43   1993
641.6′56596—dc20   93-18222

Manufactured in the United States of America on acid-free paper

9   8   7   6   5   4   3   2

First Edition

Book design by Debbie Glasserman

*With love to Rob, who inspired this work.
His enjoyment of a spoonful of peanut butter while
waiting for dinner remains a daily ritual.*

LINDA ROMANELLI LEAHY

*To my mother, Mrs. Eugene Wilson,
a wonderful cook whose peanut butter–filled
Buckeyes have been a lifelong
passion of mine.*

JACK MAGUIRE

Acknowledgments

Producing a book is a creative team effort. It begins with the author's idea and concludes with input from numerous people. Many thanks:

To Jack Maguire, friend, colleague, and occasional sparring partner;

To Faith Hamlin, agent extraordinaire for taking on this work with enthusiasm and confidence;

To Emily Bestler, editor and Virginian, who knows a good peanut idea when she sees it;

To Lee Randall, friend, writer, and first collaborator on this venture;

To Constance Costagliola, sidekick and friend for life;

To Leni Friedman, best baker I know;

To Kate and Jenna Leahy, daughters and trusted critics in matters of food and otherwise;

And to the following family members, friends, and acquaintances who have sent me their favorite peanut butter recipes, loaned me books, called with peanut butter ideas, and taste-tested when my palate flagged:

Grace Leahy, Lyn Stallworth, Mary Novitsky, Rosemary Ghosn, Liz Leahy, Ellen Sussman, Valerie Moolman, Pat Costa, Regina Costagliola, Myron and Marion Greenstone, Andrew Ramer, Rita Maloney, Ina Feurerstein, Celia Berkman, Bette Steisel, Connie Christensen,

John Staubitz, Dr. M. Fielding, Corinne Philips, Jay Cohen, and especially Edith and Joe Romanelli, otherwise known as Mom and Dad.

LINDA ROMANELLI LEAHY

It has been a delight to collaborate professionally with Linda Romanelli Leahy after many years of joyful friendship. May there be many more years to come!

I am very grateful to my agent, Faith Hamlin, my editor, Emily Bestler, and my advisers, Marc and Jeanine Silvestri, for their hard work, help, encouragement, and general high spirits in developing this book.

I am also indebted to Tom Cowan, Rita Maloney, and Andrew Ramer for their tasteful contributions to this project as well as other projects in my life.

JACK MAGUIRE

Contents

ONE

The Incredible
Edible Spread

●■▲●■▲●■▲●■▲●■▲●■▲●■▲●■▲●■▲●■▲●■▲●■▲●■▲●

The peanut is indisputably one of nature's greatest foods.
—DR. GEORGE WASHINGTON CARVER, SCIENTIST

We can't help but remember our childhoods when we think about peanut butter. Like the madeleine biscuit for French novelist Marcel Proust, the taste of peanut butter invites remembrances of things past.

In the minds of some consumers, eating peanut butter specifically evokes the longing throughout dreary hours of schoolwork for a refreshing break at lunchtime. In the minds of others, it conjures the excitement of home baking and the delicious first mouthful of batter and, ultimately, cookie. But in almost everyone's mind, it recalls the sheer sensuous pleasure of sneaking a spoonful—or a fingerful—of a nearly perfect substance: luscious to touch, tantalizing to smell, and reassuringly hearty to taste.

For Americans in general, peanut butter has been, is, and will continue to be a touchstone to the fun and magic of youth. And so it makes sense that the best-selling brands of peanut butter in the United States have childlike names: Skippy, Jif, and the most revealing name of all, Peter Pan. But, as the recipes in this book demonstrate, there's much more to peanut butter than childhood. To paraphrase George Bernard Shaw, it's a shame that peanut butter has to be wasted on the young.

In addition to classifying peanut butter as a childhood-related food, we also tend to think of peanut butter as a quintessentially *American*

to create a certain brand-specific taste. For chunky-style peanut butter, small kernel pieces are added to the butter after grinding and represent anywhere from 10 to 25 percent of the total volume. Specialty peanut butters are also packaged in various "whipped" or "striped" combinations: e.g., with grape jelly, chocolate chips, honey, raspberries, and even cinnamon and raisins.

Old-fashioned-style peanut butter (also called "natural-style," although virtually all peanut butters consist of natural products) is made the same way but *without* the stabilizer and, in most cases, any added salt or sweetener. This gives it a somewhat coarser texture and heartier taste. It also allows the oil to separate from the butter between uses. To keep the separated oil from oxidizing (thus making the butter rancid), old-fashioned-style peanut butter should be kept refrigerated after opening.

Regular creamy- or chunky-style does *not* need to be refrigerated after opening. In fact, it may adversely affect the taste and texture.

treasure, next in line after the flag and apple pie. While there is some justification to this sentiment, it is far from accurate.

True, the product commonly known as peanut butter was invented in the United States. According to most culinary historians, a St. Louis physician concocted the spread in 1890 by grinding specially roasted peanuts in a converted meat grinder with a small amount of sugar until the mixture acquired a smooth, buttery texture. His goal was to create an easily digestible high-protein food for his elderly (and often toothless) patients. Thus, peanut butter at its conception was most intimately linked not to youth but to old age.

The name of the St. Louis inventor of peanut butter has been lost to history. However, even if he had never existed, it was clearly time for the birth of peanut butter. The very next year, a steamed nut-meal paste was developed independently by Dr. John Harvey Kellogg of Battle Creek, Michigan.

Kellogg was seeking a vegetarian source for protein rather than a source of nutrition for the elderly per se. As it turned out, his steamed product was not quite as tasty as the roasted St. Louis version. Anyway, Kellogg soon grew more interested in developing and marketing breakfast cereals with his brother—a career move that ensured *his* name, at least, would *not* be forgotten.

Meanwhile, Bayle Food Products of St. Louis purchased all commercial rights to the hometown physician's tastier spread and went on to become peanut butter's first American vendor. Like pickles, crackers, and other impulse purchases, the butter was sold locally out of grocery-store barrels, scooped into small paper trays provided by the grocer.

In 1904, Bayle officially unveiled its new delicacy to the United States, and to the planet as a whole, at St. Louis's Universal Exposition and World's Fair. The so-called peanut butter was declared a big success after it sold out in three days at a penny a sample, earning a then-noteworthy profit of $705.11.

Coincidentally, the ice cream cone and popcorn—two other famously "American" food items—also premiered at the 1904 St. Louis World's Fair. Both of these crowd pleasers were destined during the coming century to unite with peanut butter in a host of ingenious ways, including some that I have created especially for this book.

Also true about Americans' close association with peanut butter is the fact that the United States has a much higher and more rapidly rising rate of peanut butter consumption than any other nation in the world. In 1990 (the latest year for which statistics are available), Americans consumed almost four pounds of peanut butter per person, compared to two pounds per person in 1960. What's more, the figures indicate that over 40 million Americans eat peanut butter *every day,* which translates into over 800 million pounds annually: enough to cover an all-American football field 250 feet high!

Definitely *not* true, however, is the notion that peanut butter—or, more accurately speaking, the peanut in processed form—is the special property of the United States. The truth is that few other food items have found homes in as many different ethnic, regional, and national cuisines as what we in the United States call peanut butter. And many of these niches were established well before the United States even existed.

It's one of the longest, most colorful, and most culturally illuminating stories in food history. The peanut in the human diet can be traced back at least three thousand years to the Incan kingdoms of present-day Peru. Among the ruined remnants of Incan settlements dating from 1000 B.C., archaeologists have discovered peanut-shaped funerary pots containing peanut seeds and foodstuffs, each pot accompanied by its own peanut-shaped mallet. Apparently, the ancient Incans thought of crushed peanuts as heavenly fare!

For the next twenty-five hundred years, the peanut continued to be a strictly "new world" food. Then came Christopher Columbus, who tried peanuts prepared in several different ways in Haiti and even took some back to the Spanish court. Later, Hernando Cortés, the notorious conquistador, ate peanut dishes in the halls of Montezuma, ruler of Aztec Mexico. Among these dishes were a peanut paste (clearly a direct ancestor of peanut butter), flat cakes made from peanut meal, and a candy made of cracked peanuts and boiled honey. Cortés, too, considered the peanut to be a worthy present for the royals back home.

All the evidence suggests that subsequent Spanish and Portuguese visitors to Latin America came to relish peanut cuisine, for they transplanted the peanut extensively throughout newly emerging Spanish

NUTRITION IN A NUTSHELL

● ■ ▲ ● ■

A peanut is not a nut at all but a legume, or podded seed. Like beans, peas, lentils, and other legumes, peanuts are loaded with vitamins, minerals, and protein. Thus, peanut butter can make a significant contribution to a healthy, well-balanced diet, a fact that was recently underscored in the revised set of dietary guidelines adopted by the U.S. Department of Agriculture in 1992.

Peanut butter is high in calories (around 90 per tablespoon) and fat (around 75 percent). But bear in mind that a small amount of peanut butter has very large taste and nutritional benefits. And also remember that peanut butter is cholesterol free, and that most of the fat content is *unsaturated:* which means, among other things, that a small amount of peanut butter on a regular basis can actually help lower your blood cholesterol.

Specifically, one tablespoon of peanut butter supplies about 20 percent of your daily protein and niacin needs and about 10 percent of your daily need for magnesium, vitamin E, phosphorus, and copper. It is also rich in vitamin B_1 and

B₂, potassium, zinc, iron, calcium, and fiber (one tablespoon contains as much fiber as two slices of whole-wheat bread).

Peanut butter is cited as an excellent nutritional source in the dietary guidelines of the Physicians Committee for Responsible Medicine. It is also designated as an "approved food" by Weight Watchers and by the American Diabetes Association.

THE PEANUT BY ANY OTHER NAME

● ■ ▲ ● ■

Besides *goober pea* and *goober,* the peanut in American English has also been called *pinder* (derived from the African term *pindal*), *earthnut, groundnut, groundpea,* and *monkey nut.* In some parts of the country, these terms are still used.

Whatever the peanut is called, it's called quite often. Although more than half of the U.S. peanut crop goes into making peanut butter, one of the most heavily con-

and Portuguese colonies in Africa. There, it quickly evolved into a standard ingredient for soups and stews, as well as a staple in its own right.

From Africa, the peanut made its way via peanut-doting and seafaring chefs to India, Thailand, the Malay peninsula, Indonesia, the Philippines, and China. In the latter country, renowned for its sophisticated culinary tradition, the processed peanut became especially popular, not only as a topping for noodles but also as a spicy and robust additive to all sorts of main dishes, side dishes, and special snacks.

It wasn't until the slave-trading years of the seventeenth and early eighteenth centuries that the peanut was first brought into the Southeastern part of the United States, via West Africa and the Caribbean. Once here, the goober, as it was known (from the Angolan *nguba*), was remarkably slow to gain its rightful share of attention.

In part, the reputation of the peanut in the American colonies suffered from its close association with African-born slaves and with the non-Western world in general. This association made the peanut seem too proletarian and ethnic for a proper British table. But even more responsible for keeping the peanut in its lowly place was an overall lack of culinary experimentation during this period in American history. Confronted with novelty and change on so many fronts, the American colonists clung to traditional, European-based dietary habits as tightly as they could. They simply wouldn't allow themselves to envision all the wonderful eating possibilities contained within the small, pleasant-tasting but utterly foreign little peanut.

Despite winning many Yankee converts during the Civil War (its nickname inspired the well-known soldier song "Eatin' Goober Peas"), and despite charming the masses as a buttery spread at the 1904 St. Louis World's Fair, the peanut remained a Southern-based and relatively rare food item well into the twentieth century. The one exception was the roasted peanut.

Shortly after the St. Louis World's Fair, the famous circus promoter P. T. Barnum began selling roasted peanuts under the big top. To Barnum and the other promoters who copied his idea, roasted peanuts were a curious novelty that perfectly suited the fantasy image of the circus itself. The circus-going public, however, soon turned the roasted peanut into America's number one snack. They demanded roasted peanuts not only at circuses but also at baseball parks—just then proliferating across the country as baseball started turning into America's number one sport. They even demanded roasted peanuts on the street, giving rise to the sidewalk peanut vendor (colloquially known as a Mr. Peanut).

Peanut fare in general received a big boost in 1925, when Dr. George Washington Carver published a much-celebrated cookbook containing 105 peanut-oriented recipes that he'd developed and tested in his renowned botanical laboratory at the Tuskegee Institute in Alabama. During the 1920s and 1930s, Carver's cookbook went through several editions and made its way into kitchens and restaurants across the nation.

Simultaneously, peanut butter sales climbed higher and higher, and the public clamored louder and louder for a better-tasting, more conveniently packaged product. A churned, shelf-stable variety that could travel well and cook well was finally developed toward the end of the 1920s; and so peanut butter moved out of grocer barrels and into key-opened tin cans. In 1934, the year-old Skippy label debuted a "chunky-style" peanut butter, which attracted even more peanut enthusiasts.

Still, the major stimulus to peanut butter's extraordinary popularity in the United States didn't come until World War II. Throughout the war years, the U.S. government issued peanut butter to the GIs on a massive scale. It was nutritious, inexpensive, easy to pack, long-lasting, and didn't require heating or, for that matter, any elaborate preparation at all. As a bonus, the troops loved it!

In sum, peanut butter proved to be the ideal food ration for Americans overseas during the long years between 1941 and 1945; but its multiple virtues were not lost on the home front either. The low cost and widespread availability of peanut butter (now packaged in glass jars because of the wartime need for tin) prompted all sorts of peanutty permutations in American homes and restaurants—most notably involving peanut butter pie, peanut butter soup, peanut brittle, and, of course, the peanut butter sandwich.

By the end of World War II, the American public at large had acquired a lasting taste for peanut butter. This taste was passed along to

sumed snack items in America is the plain old *roasted peanut*.

Some peanuts are roasted and salted in the shell. Known as *ballpark peanuts* for their longtime popularity as a vended item in baseball stadiums, they are first soaked in salt water under pressure, then dried and roasted. However, most roasted peanuts consumed in the United States have their shells and skins removed before they are roasted and salted.

As opposed to the roasted peanut, the *dry-roasted peanut* is roasted by means of a heating process that strips the peanut of much of its oil. The dry-roasted peanut may then be either salted or left unsalted.

Finally, there is the *boiled peanut* —a much-beloved treat in the American South. Instead of being dried after picking, the peanuts are washed and boiled in salt water.

ADULT PEANUT
BUTTER LOVERS
FAN CLUB

● ■ ● ▲ ●

If you are an adult suffering from *arachibrityraphobia,* or the fear of getting peanut butter stuck to the roof of your mouth, you may not love peanut butter. But if you are among the majority of adults who *do* love peanut butter, then by all means consider joining the Adult Peanut Butter Lovers Fan Club.

Founded in 1986 by Mitch Head, executive director of the Atlanta-based Peanut Advisory Board, this unique organization boasts almost 70,000 members, including such honorary peanut-prone celebrities as Jack Nicholson, Michael J. Fox, Madonna, Dan Rather, Chris Evert, Larry King, Julia Roberts, Shirley MacLaine, and Tom Selleck. It also publishes a quarterly newsletter, *Spread the News,* that has a total circulation among over 10,000 peanut butter aficionados. During Labor Day weekend of 1990, 2,000 peanut butter lovers gathered at Disney World to commemorate the 100th anniversary of peanut butter.

To join, just mail a $3 check or

the baby boomers, who in turn passed it along to their children, and so forth. It's little wonder, therefore, that post–World War II generations are now seeking new, more imaginative, and more mature ways to indulge their inbred peanut butter cravings.

As the twentieth century turns into the twenty-first and as the focus in all aspects of life—including food—becomes increasingly cosmopolitan, peanut butter is at last coming of age in the United States. It hasn't lost its childlike charm, but it has gained an adult appeal as well. Consumers sensitive to health issues are rediscovering peanut butter as a natural food that is rich in protein, minerals, and fiber, low in sodium, and free of cholesterol—yet flavorful enough in small portions to make a legitimate, palate-pleasing contribution to low-calorie diets. Money-conscious consumers are learning to appreciate peanut butter's low cost, long shelf life, and "no-waste" usefulness. And, finally, consumers of all types, now eating more and more meals at home, are realizing peanut butter's special ability to enliven a wide variety of dishes, lending them a presence that is at once familiar and exotic, comforting and adventurous.

As tempting as peanut butter can be all by itself, it becomes even more seductive in concert with other tastes and textures. Let this book help you to help yourself to the full universe of pleasure and adventure that peanut butter offers!

OLD-FASHIONED HOMEMADE
PEANUT BUTTER

● ■ ▲ ● ■ ▲ ●

MAKES 1 CUP

Almost all of the recipes in this book can be made with the commercially produced peanut butter of your choice. In most cases, this means creamy-style peanut butter. When appropriate, a particular style of peanut butter (creamy-style, chunky-style, or old-fashioned-style) is either recommended or not recommended, given the particular taste and texture considerations of that recipe.

But why not have the fun of making your own fresh peanut butter from time to time? It's quick, easy, and distinctively delicious. The recipe below calls for unsalted nuts; however, salted nuts can also be used according to your taste preference.

2 cups unsalted dry roasted peanuts *   *1 tablespoon peanut oil (optional)*

1. Place peanuts (and oil, if desired) in blender or food processor fitted with steel blade.
2. Blend or process until mixture is thick and creamy (about 2–4 minutes). Stop machine, if necessary, to scrape down sides of container.
3. Use peanut butter immediately or refrigerate in sealed container (ideally, a glass jar). Keep refrigerated between uses. For good consistency, remove from refrigerator ½ hour before using.

* To make chunky-style peanut butter, stir ½ cup chopped peanuts into creamy-style peanut butter.

BASIC GUIDELINES FOR
COOKING WITH PEANUT BUTTER
●■▲●■▲●

• Always use room-temperature peanut butter when preparing recipes.
• When a recipe calls for peanut butter, use smooth, creamy-style peanut butter unless otherwise indicated.
• If a recipe calls for *old-fashioned-style* peanut butter, use either homemade or commercially made peanut butter that is nonhydrogenated and free of sugar or other sweeteners.
• If desired, old-fashioned-style peanut butter *may* be substituted for hydrogenated peanut butter in most recipes, unless otherwise indicated. However, keep in mind that old-fashioned-style peanut butter used in baked goods yields a slightly drier product.
• If old-fashioned-style peanut butter separates in its container (i.e., if the oil rises above the butter itself), the easiest way to reblend it is by stirring it with chopsticks. I owe this very helpful tip to my friend and colleague Andrew Ramer.
• Uncooked peanut butter tends to cling not only to the roof of your

money order and a stamped, self-addressed envelope to: the Adult Peanut Butter Lovers Fan Club, P.O. Box 7528, Tifton, Georgia 31793. Who knows? You may be able to help plan a 100th-anniversary party celebrating peanut butter's international debut at the 1904 St. Louis World's Fair!

mouth but also to cooking utensils. In part, this is because of its high protein content: as the protein oxidizes in the air, the butter bonds more tightly to the nearest surface. Therefore, after you've finished cooking with peanut butter, be sure to prewash all pots, pans, spoons, and so on with a sponge or a brush *before* putting them in a dishwasher.

BASIC GUIDELINES FOR COOKING THE RECIPES IN THIS BOOK
●■▲●■▲●

• Always read the *entire* recipe first, then gather together *all* ingredients before you begin.

• When a recipe calls for a *nonstick skillet,* consider it a strong recommendation rather than a requirement. Unless a specific recipe calls for a heavy-bottomed skillet, I prefer using a nonstick skillet because it's easy to clean and requires less cooking fat.

• I often use the term *pare* instead of its synonym *peel.* Like peel, pare means to remove the outer layer of a vegetable or a fruit with a small, sharp knife.

• *Margarine* may be substituted in recipes calling for butter.

• The term *zest* in reference to a lemon, lime, orange, or grapefruit means the outer colored portion of the rind.

• Rather than calling for the use of two *bowls* when a liquid ingredient is poured into a dry ingredient, I often call for the use of *measures* (1-cup to 4-cup, depending on the recipe step). I find liquid measuring cups more convenient, not only for pouring but also for measuring, so I use them whenever possible.

• When *preheating,* always allow at least 15 minutes for an oven and at least 10 minutes for a broiler.

BASIC GUIDELINES FOR
BAKING THE RECIPES IN THIS BOOK
● ■ ▲ ● ■ ▲ ●

• Whenever a recipe calls for *butter,* use unsalted butter for fresher flavor and for more control over the total amount of salt in the recipe (all baked goods, especially those with a high sugar content, need a little salt to balance the sweetness and to enhance the other flavors).

Be sure to use room-temperature butter, unless otherwise indicated. For example, when baking scones, chilled butter is preferable because it adds to the pastry's flakiness.

Margarine may be substituted for butter, but at a slight loss of flavor and texture.

• *Eggs* incorporate air into the batter and add structure to the final product. Always use room-temperature eggs when preparing a recipe.

• To measure *flour,* lightly spoon the flour into a measuring cup for dry ingredients, not a measuring cup for wet ingredients. Never pack it. To level it, scrape it with a knife.

• To measure a *liquid,* pour the liquid into a measuring cup for wet ingredients (one with a spout), not a measuring cup for dry ingredients. Read the measurement at eye level.

• Many of the recipes in this book call for *vegetable oil cooking spray.* Consider this a strong recommendation rather than a requirement; it's a quick and easy way to "grease" baking pans. In some recipes, however, I specifically call for buttering a pan instead of spraying it, in order to enhance the final flavor.

• *Kneading* refers to the process of manipulating dough mechanically or by hand. Essential for good bread texture, it develops the gluten in the flour, which in turn helps the dough to expand properly by allowing for even yeast distribution. The "hand method" of kneading involves pressing and turning the dough until it is smooth and elastic and no longer sticky. This usually takes about 10 minutes.

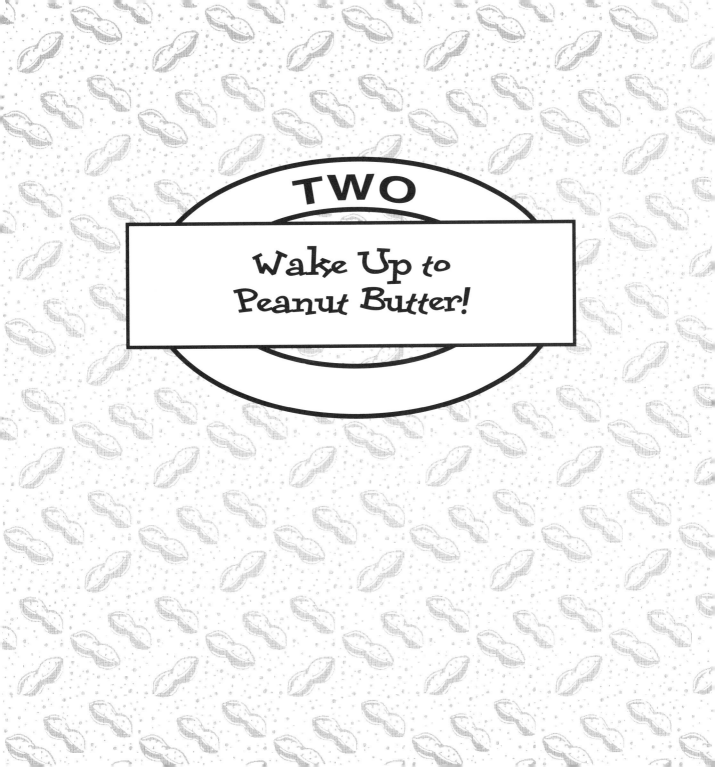

TWO

Wake Up to Peanut Butter!

To me, peanut butter is the breakfast of champions!
—GREG LOUGANIS, OLYMPIC DIVER

An easy-to-digest, high-protein, and high-comfort food, peanut butter is ideal first thing in the morning. Unfortunately, many peanut butter aficionados limit themselves at breakfast to scraping their favorite spread on a slice of toast. Fortunately, other much more stimulating possibilities will dawn on them after they have tried the recipes in this chapter.

You may want to offer your family or your guests a special surprise at breakfast—a taste of adventure that will send them into the day ahead with a smile on their lips. Or you may simply want to give yourself a soul-satisfying start to the day. Whatever your motive, you will find that a little peanut butter goes a long way toward turning routine breakfast fare into exceptionally good eating.

RAISIN BREAD BREAKFAST PUDDING

●■◆■◆●

SERVES 6–8

A hot breakfast pudding warms the heart as well as the stomach. In this version, the raisins and orange zest combine with the peanut butter to yield just the right amount of sweetness. The combination is equally

delicious cold, which makes this pudding very versatile. Top it with whipped cream, and you have an excellent, not-too-sweet dessert.

6 slices raisin bread, cut into 1-inch   *3 tablespoons dark brown sugar*
  cubes   *1 teaspoon vanilla extract*
1³/4 cups milk   *1 teaspoon grated orange zest*
4 large eggs   *(¹/4 tsp. dried orange peel)*
¹/2 cup peanut butter

1. Coat 9-inch square baking pan with vegetable oil cooking spray. Add bread cubes and set aside.

2. In blender, combine remaining ingredients. Process until smooth. Pour mixture evenly over bread cubes in baking pan, saturating bread cubes. Cover with foil and refrigerate overnight.

3. Preheat oven to 350°F. Remove foil and bake about 35 minutes, or until lightly browned and puffed.

A.M. BACON-AND-EGG QUICKBREAD

●■▲●■▲●

SERVES 4–6

Quickbread, so named because it's leavened with fast-acting baking powder and therefore "quick" to prepare, can sometimes taste as flat as it looks. By contrast, this quickbread has a robust, breakfast-in-a-bread taste.

1¹/2 cups buttermilk baking mix   *1 cup milk*
6 strips crisply cooked bacon,   *¹/3 cup peanut butter*
  crumbled   *2 large eggs*
¹/2 teaspoon freshly ground pepper

1. Preheat oven to 400°F. Coat 8-inch square baking pan with vegetable oil cooking spray and set aside.

2. In medium bowl, combine first 3 ingredients.

3. In blender, combine remaining ingredients and process until smooth. Pour liquid mixture into dry mixture and stir with a fork until just blended.

4. Spoon mixture into prepared pan, spreading evenly. Bake about 18 minutes, or until a toothpick inserted into the center of bread comes out clean.

5. Cool on wire rack for 5 minutes. Remove from pan, slice, and serve warm.

GRANOLA SUPREME

●■▲●■▲●

MAKES 6 CUPS

We have the Swiss to thank for granola, or as it's more properly called, *müesli*, German slang for "mixture." Developed in the 1890s by Swiss nutritionist Dr. Bercher-Benner, granola (*müesli*'s best-known commercial name in the United States) was meant to be a health food suitable for eating morning, noon, or night.

Served with milk at breakfast, Granola Supreme is high-octane fuel for a busy morning, but bear in mind that Granola Supreme as a topping can add a powerfully tasty punch to soups, yogurt, fruit, salads, and ice cream *any* time of the day.

3 cups old-fashioned rolled oats	*2 tablespoons peanut oil*
½ cup oat bran	*½ cup coarsely chopped unsalted*
¼ cup chopped pumpkin seeds	*dry-roasted peanuts*
½ cup peanut butter	*½ cup chopped pitted dates*
½ cup honey	*½ cup golden raisins*

1. Preheat oven to 250°F. Coat 15 × 10 × 1-inch jelly roll pan with vegetable oil cooking spray and set aside.

2. In large bowl, combine oats, oat bran, and pumpkin seeds.

3. In 2-cup measure, whisk peanut butter, honey, and oil with ½ cup water until blended. Pour over oat mixture. Stir well, until mixture is crumbly. Spread onto pan. Bake 2 hours, stirring at 15-minute intervals, until mixture is dry and crumbly. Cool on wire rack for 1 hour.

4. In medium bowl, combine peanuts, dates, and raisins. Stir into cooled mixture. Store in airtight container.

EYE-OPENER MUFFINS

●■▲●■▲●

MAKES 12 MUFFINS

Like all muffins, these taste better when warm, so leftover muffins should be heated in a toaster oven or microwaved for 15 seconds.

Like the word *butter* (especially in the phrase *peanut butter*), the word *muffin* is a very imprecise term that changes meaning according to where you are, who is cooking, and who has written the recipe. Generally speaking, the American muffin is a raised, sweetened quickbread, akin to what the Scots call a scone. It's not to be confused with the English-style muffin, which is a flat, spongy, unsweetened bread. And the English-style muffin, in turn, is not to be confused with what Americans call an "English muffin," which is only a distant relative by marriage to the English-style muffin.

The addition of chunky-style peanut butter to these muffins makes them decidedly American—and decidedly mouth-watering. When eating, make sure to pull the muffin apart instead of cutting it. That's the best way to release its tantalizing aroma and to appreciate its richly varied texture.

1 cup oat-flake cereal with raisins, crushed
1 cup all-purpose flour
1/2 cup whole-wheat pastry flour
1/2 cup chopped tart, red dried cherries or dried apricots
1/4 cup sugar
1 tablespoon baking powder
1 teaspoon ground cinnamon
1/4 teaspoon salt
1 1/4 cups milk
3/4 cup chunky-style peanut butter
1 large egg
1 teaspoon vanilla extract

1. Preheat oven to 400°F. Coat twelve 2 3/4-inch muffin cups with vegetable oil cooking spray. Set aside.

2. In large bowl, combine dry ingredients. In blender, combine milk, peanut butter, egg, and vanilla. Process until smooth. Add to dry ingredients and stir with a fork until just combined.

3. Divide batter evenly among prepared cups. Bake about 20 minutes, or until toothpick inserted in center of muffin comes out clean.

4. Cool on a wire rack for 5 minutes. Remove from pan and serve warm.

FAMILY FRENCH TOAST STICKS

●■▲●■▲●

SERVES 4–6

What we call French toast the French themselves call *pain perdu,* or "lost bread," referring to bread that is too stale to eat all by itself. As it happens, France produces more *pain perdu* than most countries. Because French bread is relatively light compared to other breads, it stales faster.

Instead of stale bread, Family French Toast Sticks calls for firmly textured white bread. A delectable finger food, these toast sticks may not be made of traditional "lost bread," but they are bound to disappear quickly at the table.

3 tablespoons unsalted butter,
    divided
3 large eggs
1/2 cup orange juice
1/4 cup peanut butter

1/2 teaspoon vanilla extract
1/4 teaspoon ground nutmeg
8 slices firm-textured white bread
Confectioners' sugar to garnish

1. Melt 1 tablespoon butter in 12-inch, nonstick skillet over medium heat.

2. In blender, combine next 5 ingredients. Process until smooth. Pour mixture into shallow bowl.

3. Stack 8 bread slices evenly on top of each other. With serrated knife, cut through stack lengthwise into 4 parallel strips, each strip about 1 inch wide. The result will be 4 side-by-side stacks of 8 sticks (yielding 32 sticks altogether).

4. Press each stick into egg mixture, coating both sides. Cook each stick 2–3 minutes on each side until golden, adding more butter to skillet as needed. Sprinkle sticks with sugar and serve.

BREAKFAST BAGEL SPREAD

●■▲●■▲●

MAKES 1¹⁄₃ CUPS

If you think peanut butter tastes good on toast and cream cheese tastes good on a bagel, wait until you try this blend of peanut butter and cream cheese on a bagel! It's also luscious dabbed on apple or pear slices, or used as a sandwich spread.

If desired, low-fat or nonfat cream cheese may be substituted for regular cream cheese.

¹⁄₂ cup peanut butter
¹⁄₂ cup cream cheese at room temperature
³⁄₄ teaspoon ground cinnamon
¹⁄₃ cup raisins
¹⁄₄ cup finely chopped shredded carrot

1. In medium bowl, combine peanut butter, cream cheese, and cinnamon.

2. Fold raisins and carrot into peanut butter mixture. Refrigerate, covered, until ready to use.

PEANUT PANCAKES WITH
MAPLE–PEANUT BUTTER SYRUP

●■▲●■▲●

MAKES 12 PANCAKES

Peanut Pancakes with Maple–Peanut Butter Syrup make a hearty breakfast dish, perfect to start off an active day or to satisfy big appetites in a big way. The batter is relatively thick, so 2 pancakes per person should be plenty. You can make more syrup if desired, but in my opinion, the richness of the pancake means that it doesn't need as much syrup as a regular pancake.

Peanut butter can easily burn, so don't forget to stir the syrup frequently while cooking.

PANCAKES

1¹⁄₂ cups milk
2 large eggs
1 tablespoon unsalted butter, melted
¹⁄₂ teaspoon vanilla extract
2 cups all-purpose flour
2 tablespoons finely chopped salted dry-roasted peanuts
1 tablespoon sugar
2 teaspoons baking powder

SYRUP (1 CUP)

*¹/₂ cup old-fashioned-style peanut
    butter*

¹/₂ cup pure maple syrup

2 tablespoons unsalted butter

Oil to coat griddle

1. To prepare pancakes, whisk first 4 ingredients in 8-cup measure or large bowl until blended. In medium bowl, combine flour, peanuts, sugar, and baking powder. Whisk dry ingredients into liquid until just blended. Let rest, refrigerated and covered, for 30 minutes.

2. To prepare syrup, combine all ingredients in small saucepan over low heat. Stir frequently until smooth. Cover and keep warm.

3. Preheat griddle or large, heavy skillet over medium-high heat. Brush griddle or skillet surface evenly with oil. Pour heaping ¹/₄ cup of batter onto hot griddle or skillet to make 4-inch pancake. Cook 3–4 minutes. Turn and cook 2 minutes longer, until golden. Repeat process with remaining batter, brushing with oil as needed. Serve piping hot with syrup.

Pancake batter should always be lightly mixed and then refrigerated for at least 30 minutes. Otherwise, the gluten in the flour develops, resulting in a tougher pancake. The resting time also relaxes tiny lumps of flour still in the mixture, rendering the pancake even lighter.

HUEVOS RANCHEROS WITH
PEANUT BUTTER SALSA

● ■ ▲ ● ■ ▲ ●

SERVES 4

From a bread paste in the halls of Montezuma to Huevos Rancheros with Peanut Butter Salsa in American breakfast nooks, peanut butter and Mexico have been close amigos. This dish turns breakfast or brunch into a full-fledged fiesta, especially when accompanied by fresh tropical fruits, like mangoes, papayas, or kiwis. For a crowd of eight, simply double the recipe. For a large and hearty North American brunch, consider serving this dish with a succulent Smithfield ham, a Virginian delicacy that owes much of its distinctive flavor to the peanut-rich diet of the pigs.

To peel tomatoes, place them in boiling water 2–3 minutes until the skin softens. Remove them from the water with a slotted spoon and place them in iced water for 1 minute. Remove and peel. Many people like to seed tomatoes, but I feel that it's unnecessary in a hearty salsa like this one.

1 cup (2 medium) chopped, peeled
   tomatoes
¼ cup finely chopped white onion
¼ cup chopped cilantro (coriander)
2 tablespoons old-fashioned-style
   peanut butter
¼ teaspoon salt
⅛ teaspoon ground red pepper

1½ tablespoons vegetable oil
4 corn tortillas
4 eggs
½ cup shredded Monterey Jack
   or cheddar cheese
Avocado slices and cilantro sprigs
   to garnish (optional)

1. Preheat oven to 200°F for 15 minutes. Turn off.

2. To prepare salsa, combine tomatoes, onion, cilantro, peanut butter, salt, and pepper in small saucepan. Place saucepan over very low heat to keep mixture warm.

3. In 12-inch, nonstick skillet, heat oil over medium-high heat. Fry tortillas 4–5 seconds on each side to soften. Reduce heat to medium. Wrap each tortilla between 2 sheets of paper towel. Stack wrapped tortillas on serving plate and put plate in oven to keep warm.

4. In same skillet, fry eggs until set (about 2 minutes). Gently turn them over and cook 15 seconds longer.

5. To assemble huevos rancheros, remove paper towels from each tortilla. Place each on its own serving plate. Top each with one egg. Sprinkle cheese evenly over each egg yolk. Spoon ¼ cup salsa around each egg white. If desired, garnish plate with avocado and cilantro. Serve immediately.

BLUEBERRY BISMARK

●■▲●■▲●

SERVES 2–4

Although blueberries taste especially good with peanut butter, any other berry can be substituted in this recipe.

An eye-catching German elaboration on the pancake, the Bismark is named for Otto von Bismarck-Schönhausen, the brilliant diplomat who engineered the unification of Germany in 1871. Blueberry Bismark is a worthy tribute to its namesake. It makes a classy breakfast or brunch dish, with a rich peanut butter flavor that will earn unanimous raves.

FILLING

2 cups fresh blueberries, rinsed and   1 teaspoon grated orange zest
    drained   1 tablespoon unsalted butter
2 tablespoons sugar

PANCAKE

2 large eggs   2 tablespoons sugar
1/2 cup milk   1/8 teaspoon salt
3 tablespoons peanut butter   Confectioners' sugar to garnish
1 teaspoon vanilla extract   (optional)
1/4 cup all-purpose flour

1. To prepare filling, combine blueberries, sugar, and orange zest in medium bowl. Set aside.

2. Preheat the oven to 425°F. Add butter to medium (10-inch) ovenproof skillet. Set aside.

3. To prepare pancake, in small bowl of electric mixer beat eggs at high speed until foamy and bright yellow (about 3 minutes). Reduce speed to medium. Add milk, peanut butter, and vanilla. Beat until blended. With machine running, gradually add flour, sugar, and salt. Beat until smooth.

4. Place skillet with butter in hot oven for 2 minutes. When butter is melted, pour batter into skillet. Return the skillet to the oven. Bake 10 minutes. Spoon blueberry mixture into center of pancake. Bake an additional 12–15 minutes until puffed and browned. Garnish with sugar and serve immediately, cutting portions into pie wedges.

CHERRY COFFEE CAKE
● ■ ▲ ● ■ ▲ ●
SERVES 9

Dried fruits are a special boon to bakers. Not only do dried fruits allow bakers to use cherries, blueberries, and cranberries when the fresh versions are unavailable but also, when combined with dry ingredients,

If the handle on your skillet is not ovenproof, cover the handle with a triple thickness of foil.

dried fruits remain buoyant in the batter instead of sinking to the bottom.

This coffee cake harmonizes the tartly sweet taste of cherries with the tangy taste of peanut butter. Nevertheless, purists who want their coffee cake to be more like the original Austrian-style coffee cake may prefer to omit the cherries. Either way, this coffee cake is *wunderbar*!

STREUSEL

¹/₃ cup all-purpose flour
¹/₄ cup plain, dry breadcrumbs
3 tablespoons chopped salted
   dry-roasted peanuts

3 tablespoons sugar
³/₄ teaspoon cinnamon
3 tablespoons unsalted butter

BATTER

2 cups all-purpose flour
¹/₂ cup sugar
2¹/₂ teaspoons baking powder
¹/₄ teaspoon salt
¹/₂ cup dried red tart cherries
³/₄ cup milk

¹/₂ cup peanut butter
¹/₄ cup (¹/₂ stick) unsalted butter,
   melted and cooled
2 large eggs
1 teaspoon vanilla extract

1. Preheat oven to 350°F. Coat an 8- or 9-inch baking pan with vegetable oil cooking spray. Set aside.

2. To prepare streusel, combine first 5 ingredients in medium bowl. Cut in butter with pastry blender until mixture resembles coarse crumbs. Set aside.

3. To prepare batter, combine flour, sugar, baking powder, and salt in medium bowl. Fold in cherries. In 4-cup measure, combine remaining ingredients. Stir liquid into dry ingredients until just blended.

4. Spread batter into prepared pan. Sprinkle streusel evenly over batter. Bake 35 minutes, or until toothpick inserted into center of cake comes out clean. Cool in pan on wire rack (about ten minutes).

PEANUT BUTTER AND JELLY SCONES

●■▲●■▲●

MAKES 11 SCONES

The scone is as Scottish as the kilt, haggis, or the sword dance. But the word itself may not be Scottish in origin. Although *scone* may have derived from the Gaelic *sgoon*, meaning "bread," or from the town of Scone, where the Scottish monarchs were crowned, the most likely derivation is the Middle Dutch expression *schoon brood*, or "fine bread."

Peanut Butter and Jelly Scones are not quite traditionally Scottish, either. Aside from the added touch of America's favorite bread-related duo—peanut butter and jelly—these scones resemble large, smooth mounds, instead of traditional scones, which are like oversized muffins. Regardless, Scots will love them just as much as, if not more than, their cherished *schoon brood*.

2 cups all-purpose flour
1/4 cup sugar
2 1/2 teaspoons baking powder
1/4 teaspoon salt
1/4 cup (1/2 stick) chilled unsalted butter, cut into pieces

3/4 cup peanut butter
1/2 cup milk
1 large egg
2 teaspoons vanilla extract
11 teaspoons grape jelly
1 egg white

1. Preheat oven to 400°F.

2. To prepare scones, combine flour, sugar, baking powder, and salt in large bowl. With pastry blender, cut in butter until mixture resembles coarse crumbs. In 4-cup measure, whisk peanut butter, milk, egg, and vanilla until blended. Stir liquid into the dry ingredients until dough forms.

3. On lightly floured surface, knead dough about 12 times until mixture is smooth. Roll into 1/4-inch thickness. With floured 2 1/2-inch cutter, make 22 rounds (use all dough). Place 11 rounds on ungreased baking sheet. Top each round with 1 teaspoon jelly; brush edges of each scone with egg white. Cover each with 1 remaining round. Gently press together, thereby sealing scone.

4. Bake 15 minutes or until lightly browned. Transfer scones with spatula to wire rack. Allow to cool slightly. Serve warm. Store in airtight container when completely cooled.

For those who prefer their scones "straight up," roll dough to a 1/2-inch thickness, instead of a 1/4-inch thickness, and do *not* add the jelly filling.

HAWAIIAN POWER SHAKE

●■▲●■▲●

SERVES 1

To give a tropical punch to your day, few drinks are as effective as the Hawaiian Power Shake. Delicious and healthy, it is also pleasing to behold, with a fresh peach color that will make sleepy eyes smile.

¹/₂ cup chopped, peeled papaya
¹/₃ cup unsweetened pineapple juice
¹/₄ cup nonfat plain yogurt
1 tablespoon old-fashioned-style
  peanut butter

1 teaspoon honey
¹/₂ teaspoon wheat germ (optional)

1. In blender, combine all ingredients. Process until smooth.
2. Add 1 ice cube. Blend until ice cube is crushed. Serve immediately.

THREE

Peanut-Perfect Appetizers and Party Pleasers

I think that I shall never see
A poem as lovely as . . . peanut butter.
—WILLIAM F. BUCKLEY, COLUMNIST

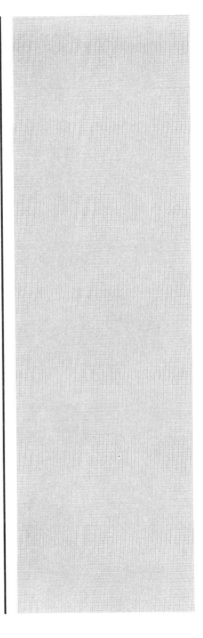

*E*xperts have a running debate about the peanut. Botanists call it a legume, like a pea or a bean. On a larger scale, this makes it a member of the rose family, along with apples, cherries, strawberries, and roses themselves. Nutritionists claim that it's a "meat" food: i.e., a rich source of protein that can substitute for beef, chicken, or pork. To consumers, however, the peanut is first and foremost a fun food—ideal for kicking off a meal or pepping up a party.

In this chapter, you'll discover a variety of dishes that help to clarify the latter point. They charm the eye as well as the palate. And they provide a welcome departure from tried-and-true—but, perhaps, tired —appetizer and party fare.

CRUNCHY VEGETABLE SPREAD
●■▲●■▲●
MAKES 1 HEAPING CUP

A vegetable spread makes an ideal light hors d'oeuvre or meal opener, especially for guests who wish to avoid meat and seafood. Unfortunately, many vegetable spreads are bland in three dimensions: taste, texture, and appearance. This sprightly spread is a standout ex-

ception in every respect! Serve it on endive leaves, small radicchio leaves, thin slices of jicama, or crackers.

1 4-ounce container whipped
cream cheese (about ¹/₂ cup)
at room temperature
¹/₃ cup chunky-style peanut butter
¹/₃ cup diced celery
¹/₄ cup sour cream

3 tablespoons minced pitted
black olives
1 tablespoon minced onion
¹/₈ teaspoon salt
¹/₈ teaspoon freshly ground pepper

1. In medium bowl, combine all ingredients until well blended.
2. Refrigerate, covered, until ready to serve. Bring to room temperature before serving.

PEANUT BUTTER HUMMUS

●■▲●■▲●

MAKES 2 CUPS

Mr. Peanut goes to the Middle East in this versatile dish. Delicious when served with pita bread triangles, endive leaves, or crudités (fresh cut vegetables), hummus delivers a full-bodied, beanlike taste with the velvety consistency of a thick cream. Traditional hummus uses tahini, a sesame seed paste that can be difficult to find in American markets. Luckily, peanut butter is a perfect substitute, producing a remarkably similar and equally satisfying taste.

Peanut Butter Hummus is easy to prepare. For a very colorful presentation, the energetic party giver may want to stuff cherry tomatoes with it. In addition to providing appetizers for about 6 people, this recipe yields 2 dinner portions, which can be set on beds of shredded lettuce surrounded by sliced tomatoes. If the hummus is refrigerated, let it stand 1 hour at room temperature before serving.

1 19-ounce can chickpeas,
rinsed and drained
¹/₄ cup water
3 tablespoons peanut butter
3 tablespoons vegetable oil

2 tablespoons fresh lemon juice
¹/₂ teaspoon salt
1 garlic clove
Paprika and chopped parsley
to garnish

1. In food processor fitted with a steel blade, combine all ingredients. Process until smooth and creamy, scraping down the sides of bowl as necessary.

2. Spoon onto a serving dish. Sprinkle with paprika and parsley.

JIFFY CHEESE STRAWS
●■▲●■▲●
MAKES 24 STRAWS

To lend a special tang to a cocktail party or a holiday feast, set out these attractive cheese straws. Reminiscent of Italian breadsticks, they're delicate, spicy, and—like any life of the party—just a little bit nutty.

*¹/₂ cup creamy-style peanut butter ** ¹/₄ teaspoon ground red pepper*
¹/₄ cup grated Parmesan cheese 1 sheet thawed puff pastry
¹/₂ teaspoon garlic powder

1. Preheat oven to 400°F.

2. In small bowl, combine first 4 ingredients until smooth.

3. On a lightly floured surface, roll puff pastry to a 14 × 12-inch rectangle. With spatula, spread peanut butter mixture evenly to the edges. Fold rectangle in half crosswise to form a 12 × 7-inch rectangle. Cut it across the width into ¹/₂-inch-wide strips. Twist each strip until a spiral forms. Place on 2 baking sheets.

4. Bake 10–13 minutes, or until lightly browned. With spatula, remove strips from baking sheets. Place on wire rack to cool. Store in airtight container.

* Old-fashioned-style peanut butter is too coarse for this dish.

Be sure to check the oven after 10 minutes of baking. Ovens fluctuate in temperature, and these straws go from a golden color to burned very quickly.

SPICY COCKTAIL PEANUTS

●■▲●■▲●

MAKES 3 CUPS

Peanuts in all their naked glory are, of course, standard party fare. But all dressed up as Spicy Cocktail Peanuts, they're anything but standard. In fact, they're downright magical. Serve these at your next party, and watch them disappear before your eyes!

¹/₃ cup peanut butter　　　　　*¹/₂ teaspoon paprika*
1 large egg white　　　　　　　*¹/₄ teaspoon ground red pepper*
2 tablespoons soy sauce　　　　*2 cups salted dry-roasted peanuts* *
1 tablespoon sugar

1. Preheat oven to 250°F.
2. In medium bowl, whisk together first 6 ingredients until smooth. Add peanuts and toss with fork to coat.
3. Spread peanut mixture on baking sheet. Bake about 30 minutes, stirring twice, until most of the nuts separate and are not sticky (leave some clumps of nuts for variety).
4. Place on wire rack to cool completely. Store in airtight container.

* The peanut butter coating will not stick to *unsalted* peanuts. They are too smooth.

MEXICAN MINIS

●■▲●■▲●

MAKES 24 MUFFINS

True to Mexico, these bite-sized muffins are spicy and festive. And they prove that big things can, indeed, come in small packages. The chunky-style peanut butter gives them a nice, crunchy texture that greatly enlarges their taste appeal.

3 large eggs
¼ cup chunky-style peanut butter
1 4-ounce can chopped mild green chilis, drained; or 1 (2-inch) jalapeño pepper, seeded and finely chopped
½ cup shredded sharp cheddar cheese

¼ cup finely chopped fresh cilantro (coriander)
3 tablespoons all-purpose flour
1 teaspoon baking powder
1 teaspoon chili powder
½ teaspoon ground cumin
¼ teaspoon salt

1. Preheat oven to 375°F. Coat two 1¾-inch mini-muffin pans with vegetable oil cooking spray. Set them aside.

2. In medium bowl, whisk together eggs, peanut butter, and chili peppers. In small bowl, combine remaining ingredients. Add dry mixture to egg mixture. Whisk until just blended.

3. Spoon mixture evenly into prepared pans. Bake 10–12 minutes, until muffins are slightly puffed and centers are set. Cool on wire rack 2 minutes. Run knife around edges to loosen muffins. Remove and serve warm.

POTATO PANCAKES AND CAVIAR

●■▲●■▲●

MAKES 24 PANCAKES

Potato pancakes, also known as *latkes,* are a traditional Jewish dish, especially popular at Hanukkah. The potato itself, however, is of South American ancestry, just like the peanut. Transported by Sir Francis Drake from the kingdom of the Incas to the kingdom of the English, the potato subsequently became a staple throughout Ireland as well as Germany and Middle Europe (where it was adopted into Jewish cuisine). From Ireland, it was carried to North America by emigrants in the early 1700s.

Now the peanut and the potato are reunited in this mouth-watering appetizer. Specifically, peanut butter, rather than egg yolk, is used as a binder for the potato pancakes. Not only does the substitution add to the flavor but it also considerably reduces the cholesterol. For a completely cholesterol-free version of this dish, eliminate both the sour cream and the caviar and serve the pancakes with applesauce.

3 medium (about 1¼ pounds)
  potatoes, pared and grated
¼ cup finely chopped onion
3 large egg whites, divided
3 tablespoons peanut butter
¼ teaspoon each salt and freshly
  ground pepper

Vegetable oil for frying
¼ cup sour cream
1 tablespoon caviar
  (the best you can afford)

1. Squeeze grated potatoes between sheets of paper towels until dry. Place potatoes in large bowl. Add onion.

2. In blender or small food processor, mix 1 egg white, peanut butter, salt, and pepper until smooth. Stir into potato mixture.

3. In small bowl of electric mixer, beat remaining egg whites at high speed until stiff peaks form. Fold into potato mixture a little at a time, until well blended.

4. In large skillet or small wok, pour oil 1 inch deep. Place over medium-high heat, until a drop of water flung on oil jumps across pan.

5. Press some potato mixture into a tablespoon. Carefully drop the tablespoonful into hot oil. Fry 1 minute on each side, or until browned. Drain on paper towels, and cover with foil to keep warm. Garnish with sour cream and caviar.

HONEY-GORGONZOLA CROSTINI

●■▲●■▲●
SERVES 6–9

Sweet Gorgonzola cheese (also known as *dolcelatte* or *Gorgonzola dolce*) gets its name from the tiny town of Gorgonzola outside Milan, Italy, but it's a world-class cheese—creamy and sweet, with a slight pungency caused by veins of natural mold. I first tried the combination of Gorgonzola and honey at Checchino dal 1887, a popular "cucina romana" restaurant in Rome's meat-packing district. Served after the main meal (as the cheese course) with a sweet marsala wine, it remains one of the most heavenly taste unions I've ever encountered.

Here I've enriched that taste union with peanut butter, and I've translated it into a topping for *crostini*. Literally, crostini are the Italian version of croutons—pieces of baked bread that are approximately slice-sized. *Buon appetito!*

18 ¹/₂-inch-thick Italian bread slices

TOPPING

6 ounces sweet Gorgonzola cheese, rind removed

2 tablespoons peanut butter

1 tablespoon finely chopped flat-leaf parsley

¹/₄ cup raw honey*

1 tablespoon finely chopped unsalted dry-roasted peanuts

18 parsley leaves to garnish (optional)

1. Preheat oven to 400°F.
2. Place bread on baking sheet. Bake 15 minutes or until golden, turning once.
3. In medium bowl, combine cheese, peanut butter, and parsley.
4. Spread thin layer of honey on each slice of bread, followed by a layer of cheese mixture. Sprinkle lightly with nuts. Place 1 parsley leaf on each slice. Serve.

* Raw honey is crystallized rather than runny. It can be found in health-food and specialty-food stores.

PEANUT BUTTER–OLIVE FOCACCIA
●■▲●■▲●
SERVES 10

The thin, chewy, peasant flatbread that northern Italians call *focàccia* (from the Latin word *focus,* or "hearth") is most familiar in this country as pizza crust. In fact, it is one of the oldest and noblest foods in the history of cooking. Remnants of carbonized focaccia have been found in the ruins of every human culture that has flourished in the lands bordering the Mediterranean Sea, clear back to Neolithic times.

Peanut Butter–Olive Focaccia is a new and worthy tribute to this time-honored bread. Simple yet savory, it is appropriate to serve all by itself or as a prelude to virtually any meal.

To make the bread in a food processor, follow these steps:

1. (See basic recipe.)

2. In food processor fitted with a steel blade, combine water, yeast, and sugar. Let stand 5 minutes. Add flour, rosemary, and salt. Pulse 3–4 times to combine.

3. In 1-cup measure, combine peanut butter and oil. With machine running, add mixture. Process dough 40 seconds to knead. On lightly floured surface, knead an additional 2–3 minutes by hand.

4. (Eliminate this step in basic recipe.)

5–9. (See basic recipe.)

DOUGH

Oil for brushing pan
1 tablespoon cornmeal
1/4 cup peanut butter
1 tablespoon peanut oil
1 cup warm water (105–115°F)
1 package active dry yeast

1/2 teaspoon sugar
3 cups all-purpose flour, divided
1 1/2 teaspoons crumbled dried rosemary
1/2 teaspoon salt

TOPPING

3 tablespoons peanut oil
2 tablespoons peanut butter

1/2 cup pitted black olives
1 teaspoon coarse salt *

1. Lightly oil a 17 × 12 × 1-inch or 15 × 10 × 1-inch baking pan. Sprinkle with cornmeal. Set aside.

2. In 1-cup measure, combine peanut butter and oil. Set aside.

3. In large bowl, combine water, yeast, and sugar. Let stand 5 minutes, until foamy. Stir in 2 1/2 cups flour, rosemary, and salt. Pour in the peanut butter mixture. Stir to form a soft dough.

4. Turn out dough onto a lightly floured surface. Knead until smooth and elastic (5–10 minutes), adding the remaining flour a little at a time.

5. Place dough in a large, oiled bowl. Turn to coat. Cover with a damp towel or plastic wrap. Let rise in a warm, draft-free place for 1 hour, or until double in size.

6. Turn dough onto prepared pan. Flatten and press dough evenly to corners of pan. Cover with towel. Let rise 30 minutes.

7. Preheat oven to 400°F.

8. To prepare topping, in 1-cup measure, whisk oil and peanut butter until combined. Pour onto the dough and spread evenly with pastry brush. Press olives into dough. Sprinkle with salt.

9. Bake 25 minutes or until crisp. Cut into 3 × 2-inch slices. Serve warm.

---

* Coarse salt is usually marketed as kosher or sea salt, which is available in many supermarkets and most specialty-food stores.

CHICKEN-LIVER SATAY

●■▲●▲●

SERVES 6

In Indonesia and Malaysia, the national dish is the *satay*, a sort of free-form shish kebab that's mildly spicy and incredibly satisfying. Whether satays are sold in a fine restaurant or on the street by a vendor cooking on a makeshift grill, they are frequently coated in a sauce made from hand-ground peanuts. Hence, I recommend here that you use old-fashioned-style or even homemade peanut butter, so that the final texture of the sauce is authentically coarse. Even though satays in general are portable, this particular satay is a sit-down appetizer, not a cocktail appetizer.

MARINADE

*½ cup unsweetened coconut milk **
2 tablespoons dark brown sugar
2 tablespoons soy sauce
2 large garlic cloves, chopped
1 tablespoon each cilantro (coriander) and cumin seeds, crushed

1 tablespoon chopped peeled gingerroot
1 teaspoon red pepper flakes
1 pound (18–21) rinsed, trimmed chicken livers

PEANUT SAUCE

½ cup old-fashioned-style peanut butter
½ cup unsweetened coconut milk
2 tablespoons soy sauce

1 tablespoon dark brown sugar
1 tablespoon chili paste †
½ teaspoon ground turmeric
½ teaspoon salt

1. In large, shallow bowl, combine all marinade ingredients. Add chicken livers, tossing to coat. Cover and refrigerate for 4 hours, turning occasionally.

2. Soak six or seven wooden skewers in water 1 hour (with 3 livers per skewer, the number of skewers depends on how many chicken livers you have).

3. Preheat grill or broiler.

Soaking the wooden skewers prevents them from accidentally burning while the satay is grilling or broiling.

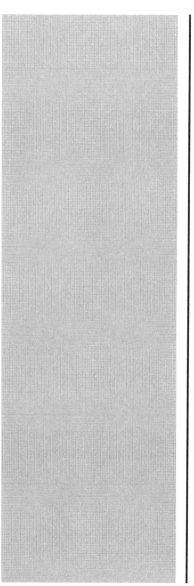

4. To prepare sauce, combine all sauce ingredients in small saucepan and stir until smooth. Stir occasionally until warm (about 10 minutes).

5. Drain chicken livers and discard marinade. Thread 3 livers onto each skewer. Grill or broil 4 inches from heat for 6–10 minutes, turning a few times until browned and slightly pink inside.

6. Place one skewer on each plate, with a heaping tablespoon of sauce on the side.

* Unsweetened coconut milk is available in many supermarkets and in most Asian markets.
** Chili paste is available in most Asian markets.

CHINESE CHICKEN WINGS
●■▲●■▲●
SERVES 6–8

Like peanuts, chicken wings are *not* just an American treat. They have their fans all over the world, especially in China. These cosmopolitan chicken wings have the peanutty spiciness characteristic of Chinese cuisine, with sufficiently sweet overtones to please the American palate. It's important to serve them warm so that this taste complexity can be fully appreciated.

12 chicken wings (about 2 pounds)
¼ cup soy sauce
¼ cup honey
3 tablespoons old-fashioned-style
  peanut butter
2 tablespoons dry sherry

1 tablespoon peanut oil
1 tablespoon cider vinegar
2 teaspoons ground star anise*
¼ teaspoon red pepper flakes
1 large clove garlic, minced

1. Preheat oven to 325°F.

2. Rinse and dry chicken. Remove wing tips and discard. Cut each wing into 2 pieces. Place wings in 9 × 13-inch baking pan. Set aside.

3. In 2-cup measure, whisk remaining ingredients until blended. Pour over wings, turning to coat. Let stand 30 minutes.

4. Bake 1 hour, turning once. With slotted spoon, remove chicken to platter. Cover with foil to keep warm.

5. Pour remaining sauce from pan into a small saucepan. Cook over high heat until liquid is reduced to ¹/₂ cup, stirring constantly.

6. Brush wings several times with sauce until all is used. Serve immediately.

* Star anise is available at many supermarkets and in most Asian markets.

CURRIED PEANUT BUTTER POPCORN

●■●▲●■▲●

MAKES 8 CUPS

Popcorn absorbs flavors beautifully and efficiently. No wonder popcorn in various flavor formats is rapidly becoming one of America's most popular party foods! Curried Peanut Butter Popcorn has an enticingly sophisticated taste: spicy with a mellow, nut-sweet undercurrent. Be sure to use old-fashioned-style peanut butter to get the full effect.

3 tablespoons unsalted butter
1 teaspoon curry powder
¹/₄ teaspoon chili powder
¹/₄ teaspoon salt

¹/₃ cup old-fashioned-style peanut butter
8 cups popcorn

1. Preheat oven to 250°F.

2. In small saucepan, combine butter and spices over low heat. Whisk until butter melts.

3. In large bowl, whisk peanut butter and butter mixture until smooth. Add popcorn, tossing gently to coat.

4. Spread popcorn mixture on 17 × 11 × 1-inch baking pan. Bake 30 minutes, stirring once.

BRUCE'S PEANUT SAUCE

●■▲●■▲●

MAKES 2 CUPS

After India, China produces and consumes more peanuts than any other nation (the United States is third). Peppery-hot peanut sauce is

Like any coated popcorn, this popcorn is slightly tacky to the touch. But it's not nearly as greasy as (for example) plain buttered popcorn.

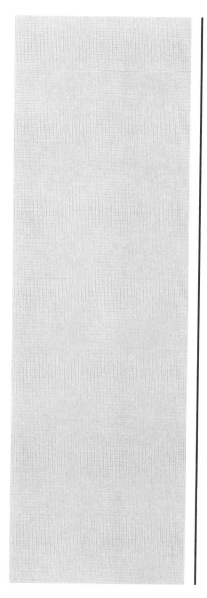

especially popular in China. For regular dining, it is served over noodles or stews. As a special appetizer, it is thinned into a dipping sauce for vegetables or chunks of cooked meat.

I created this peanut sauce in honor of my friend Bruce McIver, who makes vats of Chinese-style peanut sauce at Christmastime, both for his own use and for sending to friends as a gift. He doesn't follow a recipe, so every year the sauce tastes a bit different. Regardless, it always adds a welcome zip to the holiday season.

Bruce's Peanut Sauce is exceptionally versatile. To enjoy it as a dipping sauce, you may want to thin it with a little warm water until the desired consistency is achieved. To enjoy it as a topping, you have several alternatives. You can serve it over cooked, shredded chicken, pork, or beef that has been mounded on shredded lettuce or bok choy. Or you can simply serve it over Chinese noodles or even spaghetti. It also works deliciously well as a glaze for meats. Brush it onto the meat during the last 30 minutes of roasting.

1 cup chunky-style peanut butter
¼ cup soy sauce
2 tablespoons rice wine vinegar
2 tablespoons vegetable oil
3 tablespoons dark sesame oil
2 tablespoons dry sherry

2 teaspoons chili paste with garlic ⃰
3 tablespoons sugar
3 tablespoons toasted sesame seeds
1 tablespoon peeled, grated,
    fresh ginger with juice

1. In medium bowl, combine first 7 ingredients with ¼ cup water. Whisk sugar, sesame seeds, and ginger into mixture until combined.

2. Let stand for 2 hours to blend flavors. If not using the same day, refrigerate it. Before reusing, bring it to room temperature, adding a little warm water until the desired consistency is reached.

⃰ Chili paste with garlic is available at most Asian markets.

FOUR

Beyond the Classic Peanut Butter Sandwich

Man cannot live by bread alone.
He must have peanut butter.
—BILL COSBY, ENTERTAINER

Inevitably the first image that comes to mind when we think of a peanut butter sandwich is peanut butter and jelly on white bread. But we don't have to stop there. Now even the most conservative cook can break through this admittedly mouth-watering image to other sandwich visions—ones that can lend novel excitement to lunchtime, snacktime, or even dinnertime.

Going beyond the classic peanut-butter-and-jelly sandwich is very much in keeping with the sandwich's inventor: John Montagu, the fourth Earl of Sandwich (1718–92). His keen interest in global exploration led his friend Captain James Cook to name the Sandwich Islands (Hawaii) after him. The sandwich as a food format developed from another, related passion—gambling. On an exceptionally lucky day in 1762, the Earl of Sandwich's hand-held venison-and-bread creation allowed him to remain at his beloved gaming table for twenty-four hours straight.

In the spirit of the Earl of Sandwich, why not gamble on the alternative peanut butter sandwiches introduced in this chapter? You may just find a whole new world of sandwich enjoyment!

If desired, you can replace the banana with thin slices of your favorite fresh fruit. Strawberries, apples, pears, and peaches work especially well. You can also replace the banana with jam or jelly.

Using a nonstick skillet coated with vegetable oil cooking spray is an ideal, not a requirement. It often eliminates the need to use butter or other cooking fats and renders the skillet easier to clean.

FRUIT-FILLED
FRENCH TOAST SANDWICH
●■▲●■▲●
MAKES 2 SANDWICHES

In England, French toast is known as "poor knights of Windsor." The name goes back to a medieval distinction between the gentry—including knights—and the peasantry. The gentry typically served dessert at dinner; the peasantry did not. Poor knights (and many knights were poor) served what we call "French toast" as a simple, inexpensive, and yet suitably "rich" dessert.

While not a dessert, the Fruit-filled French Toast Sandwich is a delectable transformation of a very simple and common food item: the peanut-butter-and-banana sandwich. It makes for an impressive lunch or brunch: by yourself, with your family, or with assorted gentry.

1 large egg
1 tablespoon milk
1/2 teaspoon vanilla extract
1/4 teaspoon ground nutmeg
4 slices sandwich bread

1/4 cup peanut butter
1 small banana
2 teaspoons butter
Confectioners' sugar to garnish

1. In shallow dish, combine first 4 ingredients. Set aside.

2. Spread each slice of bread evenly with peanut butter. Slice banana and distribute slices across peanut butter side of two bread slices. Top each banana-covered slice with 1 remaining slice to make a sandwich.

3. Coat 12-inch nonstick skillet with vegetable oil cooking spray. Place over medium heat. Add butter.

4. Dip sandwich in egg mixture, carefully turning over to coat other side. Place in skillet. Repeat process with remaining sandwich. Cook sandwiches about 2 minutes on each side until lightly browned. Sprinkle with sugar and serve.

PEANUT BUTTER SANDWICH BREAD

●■▲●■▲●

MAKES 1 LOAF

Making Peanut Butter Sandwich Bread is definitely quicker and easier if you use a food processor, but you miss all the fun of kneading by hand—not to mention the healthy exercise! Whichever way you decide to make this delightfully versatile bread, the precise amount of flour you'll need may vary a bit from the stated 3½ cups. It depends on how the flour you use was milled and the humidity on the day you are baking. I prefer to use unbleached, "natural-style" flour, which is a mixture of hard and soft flours with the bran and germ removed. It tends to produce a better bread texture because of its higher gluten content.

2 teaspoons vegetable oil
1 package active dry yeast
1¼ cups warm water (105–115°F), divided
1 tablespoon honey

¾ cup peanut butter
2 tablespoons unsalted butter
3½ cups all-purpose unbleached flour, divided
½ teaspoon salt

1. Brush large bowl with oil. Set aside. In 1-cup measure, combine yeast, ¾ cup water, and honey. Let stand 10 minutes until foamy.

2. In small saucepan, combine remaining water, peanut butter, and butter over low heat. Whisk until blended. Remove from heat when temperature reaches 105–115°F, or is warm to the touch.

3. In food processor fitted with steel blade, combine 3 cups flour and salt. With machine running, add yeast mixture and peanut butter mixture. Add up to remaining ½ cup flour, as necessary, a little at a time, until mixture forms a ball. Process 40 seconds to knead. (If dough is still too sticky, add a little more flour.)

4. Place dough in prepared bowl, turning to coat with oil. Cover bowl with plastic wrap or damp towel. Let rise in a warm, draft-free place until doubled in size (about 45 minutes to 1 hour).

5. Coat a 9 × 5-inch or 8½ × 4½-inch loaf pan with vegetable oil cooking spray.

MAKING THE BREAD BY HAND

●■▲●■

1–2. Follow first two steps in original recipe.

3. Stir peanut butter mixture and the yeast mixture into a large bowl. Stir in flour with a wooden spoon, 1 cup at a time, using 3 cups. Let dough rest 10 minutes (dough will be sticky).

4. On floured surface, knead dough 10 minutes, adding remaining ½ cup of flour, a little at a time, as needed—until dough is no longer sticky but smooth and elastic.

Follow steps 4 through 7 in original recipe.

6. Punch down dough. Turn onto lightly floured surface. Shape into a 9-inch- or 8½-inch-wide rectangle (depending on loaf pan size). Roll rectangle of dough tightly, pinching ends and seams to seal. Place seam-side down in prepared pan. Cover with plastic wrap or damp towel until dough has doubled again in size (about 30 to 45 minutes).

7. Preheat oven to 450°F. Bake 10 minutes. Reduce heat to 350°F and bake 30 minutes longer, until bread is browned and bread sounds hollow when tapped on bottom. Cool in pan on wire rack.

PEANUT BUTTER DATE-NUT LOAF
●■▲●■▲●
MAKES 1 LOAF

Peanut Butter Date-Nut Loaf has a firm texture, so it's perfect when sliced thin for hors d'oeuvres, for a special lunch, or for an afternoon tea. If your tastes run to the traditional, try it with cream cheese, Brie, or Camembert. If you're more adventurous, try it with peanut butter and jelly—or as a side with scrambled eggs.

2 cups all-purpose flour
2 tablespoons sugar
2 teaspoons baking powder
½ teaspoon ground cinnamon
¼ teaspoon salt

½ cup chopped pitted dates
½ cup chunky-style peanut butter
1 cup milk
1 large egg

1. Preheat oven to 350°F. Coat a 9 × 5-inch loaf pan with vegetable oil cooking spray. Set aside.

2. In large bowl, combine first 5 ingredients. Stir in dates. In 4-cup measure, whisk remaining ingredients until blended. Pour liquid ingredients into dry. Stir until just blended. Spoon batter into prepared pan, spreading evenly. Bake 50–55 minutes. Cool in pan on wire rack for 15 minutes. Run knife around rim of pan. Remove bread and cool completely.

GRILLED CHEESE SANDWICH

●■▲●■▲●

MAKES 1 SANDWICH

According to a recent survey conducted by the *Los Angeles Times,* the peanut butter sandwich is by far the most popular sandwich in the United States—specifically, peanut butter and grape jelly, which accounts for 40 percent of all peanut butter sandwiches consumed. Third most popular (after the bologna sandwich) is the grilled cheese sandwich. This unique version of the grilled cheese sandwich lets you enjoy a combination of America's number one and number three favorites, with an unusual twist: The peanut butter is on the outside!

2 slices sandwich bread
1½ tablespoons peanut butter
1 teaspoon each butter and peanut oil

1 slice American cheese
2 teaspoons pickle relish

1. Spread 2 slices bread evenly with peanut butter.
2. In small nonstick skillet, combine butter and oil over medium heat.
3. When butter melts, add 1 slice prepared bread, peanut-butter-side down. Place cheese on top, and spread with pickle relish. Top with remaining slice of bread, peanut-butter-side up. Cook sandwich about 3 minutes on each side, until lightly browned and crisp.

GAZEBO PITA

●■▲●■▲●

MAKES 2 SANDWICHES

The United States exports more peanut butter to the Middle East than to any other area of the world. Perhaps it's because peanut butter tastes so much like tahini sauce, a very popular Middle Eastern food item, especially as a dressing in pita bread sandwiches.

The Gazebo Pita replaces tahini sauce with peanut butter in a "saucy" consistency. I named it after a similar tahini-oozing sandwich specialty at the Gazebo Restaurant, a health-food establishment that was the

heart of daily life in my neighborhood (the Park Slope section of Brooklyn, New York) during the 1970s and '80s. Served after soup, the Gazebo Pita makes a delectably light but nourishing dinner.

DRESSING

¹/₄ cup peanut butter

2 tablespoons plain nonfat yogurt

1¹/₂ tablespoons dark sesame oil

FILLING

1 cup finely shredded iceberg lettuce

¹/₂ cup nonfat cottage cheese

¹/₂ cup alfalfa sprouts

¹/₃ cup peeled, diced cucumber

¹/₃ cup sliced scallion

¹/₃ cup diced radish

2 tablespoons diced red onion

2 whole-wheat pita breads, slit at top

1. To prepare dressing, combine all ingredients with ¹/₄ cup water in blender. Process until smooth.
2. Push ¹/₂ cup lettuce into the bottom of each pita. Spoon ¹/₄ cup cottage cheese over lettuce. Divide remaining ingredients evenly between each pita, gently stuffing into pocket. Drizzle ¹/₄ cup dressing into each pocket. Serve with plenty of napkins.

OPEN-FACE ENGLISH MUFFIN

●■▲●■▲●

MAKES 2 SANDWICHES

The Open-face English Muffin is truly international in spirit, and in keeping with that spirit, feel free to cross borders as you wish. Add more peanut butter or more salsa. For an exciting jolt of hot spiciness, try the hottest salsa you can find. Or maybe you'll want to explore substitute ingredients, like pickle relish instead of salsa, or a slice of Bermuda onion instead of diced avocado.

2 English muffins, split in half and lightly toasted

4 tablespoons chunky-style peanut butter

¹/₂ cup diced avocado

8 teaspoons salsa

4 strips raw bacon, cut in half

1. Preheat broiler.
2. Spread each muffin half with 1 tablespoon peanut butter. Top each with 2 tablespoons avocado. Spoon 2 teaspoons salsa on each and top with 2 strips bacon.
3. Broil 4 inches from heat 4–5 minutes, until bacon is crisp.

REUBEN WITH NEW WORLD RUSSIAN DRESSING

●■▲●■▲●

MAKES 2 SANDWICHES

Like the English muffin, German chocolate cake, Chinese chop suey, and Italian veal parmigiana, Russian dressing is, in fact, an American creation designed to capture the essentials of a foreign cuisine in a more familiar idiom. Likewise, the Reuben is not based on an "old world" marriage of sauerkraut, corned beef, Swiss cheese, and rye bread as many Americans think it is. It was submitted to a U.S. National Sandwich Contest in 1956 by Fern Snider, an Omaha, Nebraska, waitress who named her entry after one of her clients, Reuben Kay. The Reuben sandwich won the contest, and you'll be a winner with this revamped version.

DRESSING

¹/₄ cup mayonnaise
2 tablespoons peanut butter
2 tablespoons catsup

1 tablespoon jarred diced pimento, mashed
1 teaspoon Worcestershire sauce

FILLING

4 slices Jewish rye bread with caraway seeds
1¹/₂ tablespoons softened butter
¹/₄ pound lean sliced corned beef or smoked turkey

1 cup sauerkraut, drained and squeezed, at room temperature
4 thin slices (about 2 ounces) Swiss cheese
Dill or sour pickles (optional)

1. Coat a 12-inch nonstick skillet or griddle with vegetable oil cooking spray. Set aside.

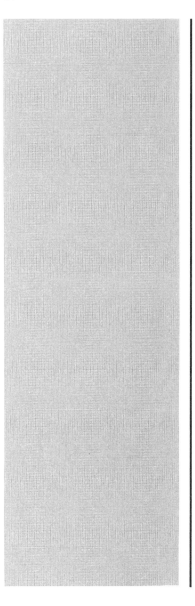

2. To prepare dressing, combine all ingredients in small bowl. Set aside.

3. To assemble sandwich, place bread slices on counter. Spread each slice evenly with butter. Turn over 2 slices, and spread each with 2 tablespoons of the dressing. Then, on top of the dressing, evenly layer (in order) corned beef or turkey, sauerkraut, and Swiss cheese. Top each with 1 slice of remaining buttered bread, buttered-side up.

4. Put prepared skillet or griddle on medium heat for 5 minutes. Add sandwiches and press down with spatula. Cook about 5 minutes on each side, until bread is browned and cheese is slightly melted. Cut each sandwich in half. Serve with remaining dressing (on the side) and pickles.

TEA SANDWICHES
●■▲●■▲●
MAKES 16 SANDWICHES

Apples, currants, and carrots make these multilayered sandwiches a scrumptious and healthy treat all by themselves or as the main attraction in a proper British tea. After all, the Duchess of Bedford began the custom of serving afternoon tea, complete with cakes or sandwiches, in 1771 for the express purpose of curing what she called the "five o'clock sinking feeling." And what better energy food is there at *any* time than peanut butter? For a full "peanut butter tea," serve these Tea Sandwiches along with Peanut Butter Date-Nut Loaf (also in this chapter), Eye-opener Muffins (in chapter 2), and assorted jams.

½ cup peanut butter
2 tablespoons softened unsalted butter
½ cup finely chopped, peeled, cored apple (1 small apple)
¼ cup dried currants

¼ cup finely chopped shredded carrot
2 tablespoons apple butter
8 slices very thin whole-wheat bread
4 slices very thin white bread
Watercress to garnish (optional)

1. In medium bowl or small food processor, combine peanut butter and butter until blended. Stir in apple, currants, carrot, and apple butter until combined.

2. Spread 4 slices wheat bread evenly with mixture. Top each wheat slice with 1 slice white bread. Spread remaining mixture evenly on white slices. Top each white slice with 1 of remaining 4 wheat slices. Press each sandwich stack firmly together.

3. Line a 9-inch square pan or airtight plastic container with damp paper towels. Place sandwiches in one layer in pan or container. Cover layer with additional damp paper towels. Cover pan or container tightly with foil or lid. Refrigerate at least one hour (up to one day) ahead.

4. To serve, cut crusts from stack with serrated knife. Cut each stack into quarters (four equal parts). On serving plate, place each quarter on its side, to show layers. If desired, place watercress in center of plate.

BAKED EGGPLANT SANDWICHES
WITH PEANUT-WALNUT SAUCE
● ■ ▲ ● ■ ▲ ●
SERVES 4

The wonderful taste and texture combination of eggplant and walnut sauce is characteristically Russian and usually found in a sumptuous main dish or side dish. Here it appears in an elegant sandwich, enhanced American-style by the addition of ham, tomato, and a touch of peanut butter.

1 medium eggplant (about 1 pound)
Salt

¼ cup all-purpose flour
Oil for frying

SAUCE

2 tablespoons walnut oil
2 garlic cloves, minced
½ cup heavy cream
½ cup chicken broth
¼ cup peanut butter

¼ cup chopped walnuts
¼ cup chopped flat-leaf parsley to garnish
Salt and freshly ground pepper to taste

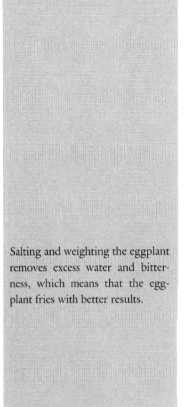

Salting and weighting the eggplant removes excess water and bitterness, which means that the eggplant fries with better results.

This is a foolproof method for cooking cornmeal without lumping. However, don't leave the kitchen once the cooking begins. It needs watching!

FILLING

*1 large tomato (about ¹/₂ pound), cut   4 thin slices boiled ham, cut in
  into 8 (¹/₈-inch-thick) slices   quarters*

1. Trim eggplant and cut crosswise into 16 (¹/₄-inch-thick) slices. Sprinkle lightly with salt on both sides of each slice. Place slices in a colander set over a shallow bowl. Place a weighted plate on top. Let drain 1–2 hours.

2. Rinse and dry eggplant slices with paper towels. Place flour on length of wax paper. Dredge each eggplant slice in flour, shaking off excess.

3. Fill large skillet with oil to ¹/₂-inch depth. Place over medium heat (375°F). Add eggplant slices, a few at a time. Fry about 4 minutes on each side, until browned. Drain on paper towels.

4. Preheat oven to 350°F.

5. To prepare sauce, heat walnut oil over low heat in medium non-stick skillet. Add garlic and cook about 3 minutes, until the garlic is soft. Whisk in cream, broth, and peanut butter until mixture is smooth. Increase heat to medium. Cook 10 minutes, whisking occasionally until sauce is thickened. Remove from heat. Add walnuts, parsley, salt, and pepper.

6. To assemble sandwiches, place 8 eggplant rounds in a 9 × 13-inch baking pan. Top each with 1 slice of tomato and 2 slices of ham. Place remaining eggplant rounds on top. Spoon sauce evenly over each sandwich. Bake sandwiches for 15 minutes until warm. Serve immediately.

MAIN-DISH

CHICKEN MOLE SANDWICHES

●■▲●■▲●

SERVES 4

From a Mexican perspective, mole is a traditional chocolate-and-chili-based sauce that ennobles chicken or turkey, especially in tacos. From a U.S. perspective, mole offers a sly hint of Mexican spiciness that is particularly pleasing to more moderate palates in a wide range of Mexican-related dishes. No matter how you look at it, though, Main-dish Chicken Mole Sandwiches will provide a substantial meal with relative ease. The chicken mole itself can be made a day in advance (add a little more chicken broth when reheating the mole if it is too thick).

For a lunch that's a fiesta, I recommend serving this sandwich with sour cream. Afterward, offer a salad with cilantro dressing: 3 parts oil, 1 part vinegar, chopped cilantro, salt, and pepper. End the meal with a dessert of grilled pineapple slices sprinkled with sugar and cinnamon.

CORNMEAL SANDWICH SLICES

3 cups water
2 cups stone-ground yellow cornmeal

1 teaspoon salt

CHICKEN MOLE

1 (3¹/2- to 4-pound) chicken
1 (14-ounce) can peeled tomatoes
  with juice
2 each, dried ancho *and* pasilla
  chilis (seeds removed; wear gloves),
  crumbled *
1 medium onion, chopped
1/2 cup salted dry-roasted peanuts
1 garlic clove

1 teaspoon sugar
1/4 teaspoon ground cinnamon
1/8 teaspoon anise extract
2 tablespoons vegetable oil
1/3 cup raisins
1 (1-ounce) square unsweetened
  chocolate
1/4 cup vegetable oil for frying
  cornmeal slices

1. Oil or spray a 7 × 12-inch baking dish and a large spatula. Set aside.

2. To prepare sandwich, in heavy 3-quart saucepan vigorously whisk all sandwich-slice ingredients until mixture is smooth. Cook over medium heat, whisking frequently. When mixture comes to a simmer, whisk often until thick and stiff (about 7–10 minutes). Immediately spoon mixture into prepared baking dish, spreading evenly with prepared spatula. Cool, cover with foil, and refrigerate at least 3 hours (or overnight).

3. Place chicken in dutch oven. Add cold water to just cover top of chicken. Bring to a simmer, uncovered, over medium heat. Poach 1 hour. Remove chicken, reserving 2 cups broth (keep remaining broth for other uses). Discard skin. Cut chicken from bones and shred. Set aside.

4. To prepare mole sauce, place next 8 ingredients in blender. Process to a coarse paste.

5. Heat oil in dutch oven over medium heat. Add paste and cook 5 minutes, stirring frequently. Add raisins, chocolate, and 1 cup broth. Stir until chocolate melts (about 3 minutes). Add chicken. Reduce heat to low. Cover and cook 45 minutes, adding remaining 1 cup broth as needed.

6. Invert cold cornmeal onto large cutting board. Wet a large knife with water. Cut cornmeal into 8 slices, approximately $3 \times 3\frac{1}{2}$ inches.

7. Heat oil in a 12-inch nonstick skillet over medium-high heat. Fry a few cornmeal slices at a time, about 5 minutes on each side, until browned. Drain on paper towels.

8. Place 1 slice cornmeal on each serving plate. Cover each slice with 1 heaping cup mole. Then top each slice with remaining slice and any remaining mole.

* Dried *ancho* and *pasilla* chilis are available at Mexican markets and specialty-food stores.

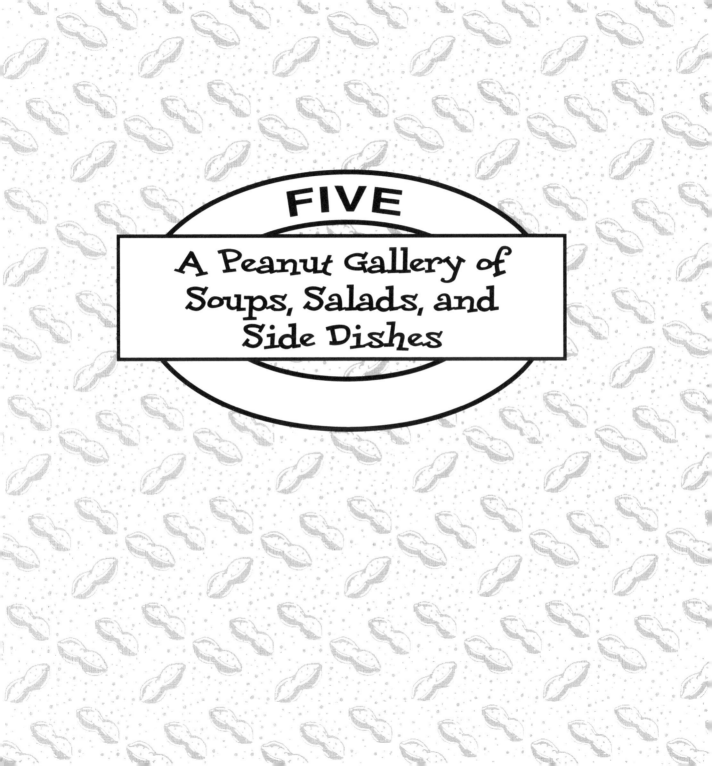

FIVE

A Peanut Gallery of Soups, Salads, and Side Dishes

All day long you'll find me
Eatin' goober peas.
        —CIVIL WAR SONG

Conservative cooks may want to begin here to appreciate peanut butter's multifaceted taste and texture attributes. There's nothing like a dash of peanut butter to give a soup, salad, or side dish a zesty life of its own. This is especially true regarding vegetables, which are often underappreciated and overlooked by cooks and diners alike.

Enlivening any small dish—vegetable or not—with peanut butter is an easy and imaginative way to bring more flavor, nutrition, and all-around excitement into one's daily diet. In this chapter, you'll find a wide world of choices to suit a variety of different dining situations.

AFRICAN PEANUT SOUP

•■▲•■▲•

SERVES 6

The spicy tingle of peanut soup is one of the distinctive tastes of West African cooking. This American adaptation captures that exquisite taste in a thick, rich, winter-style soup. It's hearty enough to serve as a main dish yet blissfully easy to prepare.

2 tablespoons vegetable oil
2 red bell peppers, seeded and
　chopped
2 medium onions (about 2 cups),
　chopped
3 garlic cloves, mashed
4 cups chicken broth (preferably
　homemade)

1 (28-ounce) can crushed tomatoes
1/2 teaspoon freshly ground black
　pepper
1/2 teaspoon ground red pepper
2 cups cubed cooked chicken
1/2 cup raw rice
1 cup old-fashioned-style peanut
　butter

1. In large dutch oven, heat oil over medium-high heat. Add peppers, onions, and garlic. Cook 10 minutes, stirring frequently, until vegetables are lightly browned and wilted.

2. Reduce heat. Add broth, tomatoes, spices, and 4 cups water. Simmer, uncovered, for 45 minutes, stirring occasionally.

3. Add chicken and rice. Cook 20 minutes. Whisk in peanut butter until well blended. Cook 10 minutes longer, stirring occasionally.

COLONIAL PEANUT BUTTER SOUP

●■▲●■▲●

SERVES 8

We know that America's founding fathers and mothers in Virginia, North Carolina, South Carolina, and Georgia were familiar with the peanut. Well before Thomas Jefferson became president of the United States, he was growing peanuts at Monticello. What we do *not* know is whether residents of colonial America actually made peanut butter soup. If they didn't, they certainly should have!

Colonial Peanut Butter Soup is very much like the types of soups that are known to have been prevalent in the southern colonies. In fact, a similar version of this soup is served at the King's Arms Tavern in Williamsburg, Virginia. To top it off handsomely and semihistorically, try Herbed Peanut Butter Croutons (page 59).

6 tablespoons unsalted butter
2 stalks (about 1 cup) diced celery
2 medium (about 1 1/4 cups) diced,
　pared carrot

6 cups chicken broth (preferably
　homemade)
2 cups peanut butter
1/2 cup plain yogurt

1 medium (about 1 cup) diced,
* pared parsnip*
1 medium (about 1 cup) diced,
* rinsed leek, white part only*

Freshly ground pepper to taste
Herbed Peanut Butter Croutons to
* garnish (optional) (see below)*

1. In a large dutch oven, melt butter over medium-high heat. Add the vegetables. Cook 3 minutes, cover the pot, and cook 7 minutes longer, stirring frequently. Remove the vegetables with a slotted spoon. Place half the vegetables in a food processor fitted with a steel blade. Process to a puree. Return the puree to the pot. Set aside the remaining vegetables.

2. Add broth to the pot. Bring to a boil over medium-high heat. Reduce the heat to low. Whisk in peanut butter and cook 5 minutes. Add the remaining vegetables and the yogurt. Cook 5 minutes longer or until heated through.

HERBED PEANUT BUTTER CROUTONS

●■▲●■▲●

MAKES 4 CUPS

According to food historians, croutons—a French invention—originated as pieces of bread crust *(croûte)* served with game or poultry after being fried in the game or poultry drippings. Now cooks around the world make croutons in a variety of different ways for a variety of different purposes.

Herbed Peanut Butter Croutons are baked rather than fried, in a seasoned peanut butter mixture, and they are made from the bread itself rather than the crust. They go especially well sprinkled on top of Colonial Peanut Butter Soup (page 58). But, like most good croutons, they can be served atop virtually any soup, salad, or puree, as well as chicken fricassee or scrambled eggs.

When preparing these croutons, be sure to use a bread with a firm texture, not a soft, sandwich-style bread. This will ensure that the croutons remain crisp for a longer period of time. Also, be sure to use old-fashioned-style peanut butter. It yields a stronger peanut flavor.

¹/₃ cup peanut oil
¹/₄ cup old-fashioned-style peanut butter

2 teaspoons dried tarragon (or herb of choice)
8 slices firm-textured bread, crusts removed

1. Preheat oven to 400°F. Oil a 15 × 10 × 1-inch jelly roll pan. Set it aside.

2. In small bowl, combine oil, peanut butter, and herbs. Brush one side of each bread slice with mixture. Place each slice, peanut butter side down, on prepared pan. Brush top of each slice with remaining peanut mixture. To form cubes, cut each slice lengthwise into six ¹/₂-inch-thick strips. Cut each slice again, crosswise, into six strips. Separate cubes with a fork.

3. Bake 8–10 minutes or until crisp and browned, stirring occasionally. Cool completely on wire rack. Store in airtight container.

The amount of chili paste may be reduced to 1 teaspoon if a milder flavor is desired.

SINGAPORE SALAD
●■▲●■▲●
SERVES 8

Mixing vegetables and fruits in a single dish is characteristic of Singaporean cuisine, which is slightly different from Malaysian cuisine, and so is adding a dash of peanut butter. This very refreshing and spicy Singapore-style salad makes a great summer side dish. It's especially compatible with grilled fish.

DRESSING

¹/₄ cup hoisin sauce
¹/₄ cup tofu
2 tablespoons old-fashioned-style peanut butter

2 tablespoons lime juice
1 tablespoon soy sauce
*2 teaspoons chili paste with garlic **
1 teaspoon sugar

SALAD

*2 cups (5 ounces) snow peas,
   trimmed*
*1 small mango, peeled, pitted, and
   cut into small chunks*
*1 small papaya, peeled, pitted, and
   cut into small chunks*
*½ small pineapple, peeled, cored, and
   cut into small chunks*

*1 (8-ounce) can sliced water
   chestnuts, drained*
*2 tablespoons coarsely chopped,
   unsalted dry-roasted peanuts, to
   garnish*

1. To prepare dressing, combine all ingredients with 2 tablespoons water in blender. Process until smooth.

2. In large bowl combine all salad ingredients. Pour dressing over mixture and toss to coat. Spoon onto serving platter. Sprinkle with peanuts.

* Chili paste with garlic is available at most Asian markets.

NEW POTATO SALAD

●■▲●■▲●

SERVES 4

During the second half of the nineteenth century, the number of German immigrants into the United States soared, and so did the American love affair with potato salad—or, as the Germans call their native creation, *Kartoffelsalat*. Since then, more and more Americans have substituted mayonnaise for the original dressing of olive oil and vinegar.

New Potato Salad goes one step further, replacing the mayonnaise with a light peanut butter dressing that will make you fall in love with potato salad all over again. Throw out the mayonnaise—and with it the cholesterol!

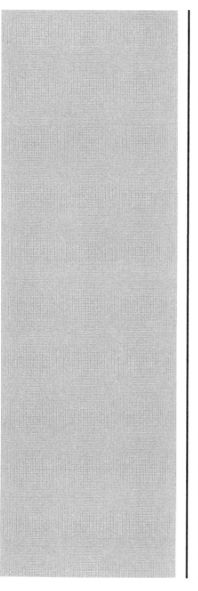

*1¹/₂ pounds red new potatoes, washed
  and scrubbed*
¹/₂ cup chicken broth
¹/₄ cup peanut butter
¹/₄ cup chopped fresh basil
2 tablespoons white vinegar

¹/₂ teaspoon salt
¹/₄ teaspoon freshly ground pepper
¹/₃ cup diced red onion
3 large hard-cooked egg whites
*¹/₄ cup chopped pimento-stuffed green
  olives*

1. Place potatoes in large pot of boiling water. Reduce heat to medium-high. Cover and cook 20–25 minutes, or until potatoes are tender when pierced with a fork.

2. To prepare dressing, whisk together broth, peanut butter, basil, vinegar, salt, and pepper in a 2-cup measure until blended. Set aside.

3. Drain, cool, and quarter potatoes. In medium bowl, combine potatoes with onion, egg whites, and olives. Pour dressing over the potato mixture. Toss to coat.

FIDDLEHEAD FERN
AND WHITE BEAN SALAD
●■▲●■▲●
SERVES 4

Look at *any* fern frond when it has just poked through the soil, and its shape will remind you of the head of a fiddle. Picked, cooked, and eaten, the head of the ostrich fern in particular—tasting a little like green beans with a mushroom undertone—makes music in your mouth. Most specialty markets, and some supermarkets, stock fiddlehead (ostrich) ferns from late March until the end of June.

Fiddlehead Fern and White Bean Salad is as fresh and lively as a spring melody, and if you or your guests haven't previously tried fiddlehead ferns, it's a wonderful introduction. For a special meal, serve the salad with room-temperature lamb, another sprightly springtime dish.

¹/₂ pound fiddlehead ferns, washed
and trimmed (about 4 cups)
3 tablespoons peanut butter
2 tablespoons balsamic vinegar
1 tablespoon chopped fresh rosemary
(³/₄ teaspoon dried)
¹/₄ teaspoon salt

¹/₄ teaspoon freshly ground pepper
1 cup canned cannellini (Great
Northern) beans, drained and
rinsed
¹/₄ cup minced shallot
4 large radicchio leaves to garnish

1. In medium pot of boiling water, cook ferns about 5 minutes, or until tender when pierced with a fork. Drain.

2. To prepare vinaigrette, in 1-cup measure, combine peanut butter, vinegar, rosemary, salt, and pepper with ¹/₄ cup water.

3. In large bowl, combine ferns, beans, and shallots. Pour vinaigrette over mixture. Toss to coat. Place each radicchio leaf on a plate. Spoon a heaping cupful of mixture onto each leaf.

PEANUT BUTTER–BANANA FRITTERS

●■▲●■●

MAKES 18 FRITTERS

Peanut Butter–Banana Fritters is adapted from a recipe used at Goodfellows, a deservedly famous restaurant in Minneapolis, Minnesota. As a side dish, these slightly crunchy fritters offer an unusual and excellent variation of the familiar peanut butter-and-banana taste combination. Serve them with grilled fish, chicken, or pork.

Vegetable oil for frying
1 cup all-purpose flour
1 tablespoon sugar
1 teaspoon baking soda
¹/₄ teaspoon salt

³/₄ cup milk
1 large egg, lightly beaten
¹/₂ cup chunky-style peanut butter
1 medium banana, chopped

1. In 3-quart saucepan, small wok, or electric skillet, pour vegetable oil to a depth of 1 inch. Heat to 350°F.

2. In large bowl combine flour, sugar, baking soda, and salt. Whisk in milk and egg until batter is smooth. Whisk in peanut butter until blended. Fold in banana.

The temperature of heated oil fluctuates. If the fritters appear to be browning too quickly, reduce the heat. If using a deep fryer, follow the manufacturer's instructions.

3. Carefully drop batter into the hot oil, a tablespoonful at a time. Fry fritters, turning occasionally, until golden brown (3–4 minutes). Drain well on paper towels.

HERBED POTATO GRATIN
●■▲●■●
SERVES 6

A *gratin* is uncomplicated to prepare yet marvelously rewarding to serve and to eat. Basically, it involves putting food into a baking dish and topping it with some sort of sauce, cheese, and/or crumb mixture that will form a crust, thus sealing in the food's flavor and moisture.

Herbed Potato Gratin, unlike many potato gratins, does not use egg or heavy cheese in the topping. Instead it relies on skim milk and low-fat cottage cheese, with peanut butter as a binder and flavor enhancer. This makes it not only delicious, with a slight hint of peanut, but also much lower in cholesterol.

The finished dish cuts into perfect wedges and is a terrific brunch item served with scrambled eggs. It's good even at room temperature. What's more, it's hearty and tasty enough to make a great vegetarian main dish (serving 4).

1 16-ounce container low-fat cottage cheese
1/2 cup skim milk
1/4 cup peanut butter
2 tablespoons chopped fresh rosemary (2 teaspoons dried)

1/2 teaspoon salt
1/4 teaspoon freshly ground pepper
1 1/2 pounds potatoes, washed and scrubbed

1. Preheat oven to 400°F. Coat 11 × 7 1/2-inch baking pan with vegetable oil cooking spray. Set aside.

2. In large bowl, whisk all ingredients except potatoes, until blended.

3. Slice potatoes (with skin) into 1/8-inch-thick rounds. Arrange rounds in single layer in prepared pan. Spoon cheese mixture evenly over rounds. Repeat procedure with remaining rounds and cheese mix-

ture, ending with layer of cheese mixture. (There will be 4 layers altogether.)

4. Bake 45–50 minutes, until potato rounds are tender when pierced with a fork and top cheese layer is browned and crisp.

RISOTTO WITH BALSAMIC VINEGAR

● ■ ▲ ● ■ ▲ ●

SERVES 4

When it's prepared correctly, *risotto* (from the Italian *risetti,* or "little rice") is a uniquely tasty first-course dish that enraptures devotees of Italian cooking. The magic lies in the texture of the rice. The rice kernel must be *al dente,* literally "to the tooth," which means that it must have a certain degree of bite without being hard. Aside from this requirement, risotto is a very simple and easy dish.

Risotto with Balsamic Vinegar features arborio rice, a short-grain rice grown in the Po Valley of northern Italy and widely available in specialty-food stores. When cooked properly, the outside of arborio rice softens and becomes creamy when stirred. As a result, it complements almost any ingredient, including shellfish, vegetables, cheese, and herbs. Other rices don't have the same reaction or result, so avoid substitutions!

I particularly recommend this risotto as a side dish with fresh ham and carrots or cinammon-baked acorn squash, accompanied by a crisp Riesling wine. It's slightly acidic, so when serving it with a salad, use a mild, creamy dressing rather than a vinaigrette.

5 cups beef broth
¼ cup olive oil, divided
8 ounces (3 cups) sliced Cremini (brown) mushrooms
¼ cup balsamic vinegar
¼ cup peanut butter

¼ cup minced onion
1 cup Arborio rice
¼ cup chopped, fresh flat-leaf parsley
¼ teaspoon freshly ground pepper
¼ cup chopped, unsalted dry-roasted peanuts (optional)

1. In medium saucepan, heat broth to just below a simmer.
2. In medium skillet, heat 2 tablespoons oil over medium heat. Add

mushrooms and sauté until golden (about 10 minutes). Remove mushrooms with a slotted spoon. Place in medium bowl. Cover and keep warm.

3. Combine vinegar and peanut butter in skillet, stirring until blended and smooth. Add mixture to mushrooms. Toss to coat. Cover and keep warm.

4. In large, heavy saucepan or dutch oven, heat remaining oil over medium heat. Cook onion 2–3 minutes until soft. Stir in rice until well coated.

5. Add ½ cup warm broth to rice, stirring constantly until liquid is absorbed. Repeat procedure until all broth is used and rice is tender but not mushy (20–25 minutes). Stir in mushroom mixture, parsley, and pepper. Garnish with peanuts, if desired. Serve immediately.

SWEET-POTATO SOUFFLÉ
WITH GINGERED BOURBON SAUCE
●▪▲●▪▲●
SERVES 8

The word *soufflé* itself is derived from the French *souffler,* meaning "to breathe, puff, or blow." In culinary language, it refers to any dish that lifts itself beyond the confines of its dish while baking—thanks to the air incorporated into the beaten egg whites.

This dish is an especially happy marriage of French and southern U.S. cooking that lifts the taste of peanut butter to new heights. For an alcohol-free but still very tangy sauce, simply omit the bourbon.

SOUFFLÉ

1 pound (2 medium) sweet potatoes,
  pared and cut into chunks
¼ cup peanut butter
3 tablespoons unsalted butter
1 cup skim milk
6 large eggs, separated

1 teaspoon grated orange zest
½ teaspoon salt
½ teaspoon ground nutmeg
¼ teaspoon freshly ground pepper
¼ teaspoon cream of tartar

SAUCE

1 tablespoon vegetable oil   *6 tablespoons peanut butter*
1 tablespoon minced gingerroot   *1 tablespoon sugar*
1¹/₄ cups orange juice   *2 tablespoons bourbon*

1. In medium saucepan, combine potatoes and enough water to cover potatoes. Bring to a boil over medium-high heat and cook 15–20 minutes, until tender. Drain.

2. Preheat oven to 375°F.

3. In food processor fitted with a steel blade, combine potatoes, peanut butter, and butter. Process until smooth. Add milk, 4 egg yolks (discard remaining yolks), and spices. Pulse 20 times. Transfer mixture to a large bowl.

4. In large bowl of electric mixer, beat egg whites at medium-low speed until frothy. Add cream of tartar and beat at medium-high speed until soft peaks form. Gently fold egg whites a little at a time into potato mixture until well blended, leaving no white streaks of beaten egg whites.

5. Spoon mixture into 6-cup soufflé dish. Place dish in 9 × 13-inch baking pan; place on oven rack. Pour boiling water into baking pan to cover halfway up side of soufflé dish. Bake about 50–55 minutes, until puffed and browned but slightly jiggly in the center.

6. To prepare sauce, in medium skillet heat oil over medium-high heat. Add ginger and sauté until browned (about 1 minute). Carefully pour in orange juice. Whisk in peanut butter and sugar. Simmer about 15 minutes or until sauce is slightly reduced, whisking frequently. Add bourbon and cook 1 minute longer.

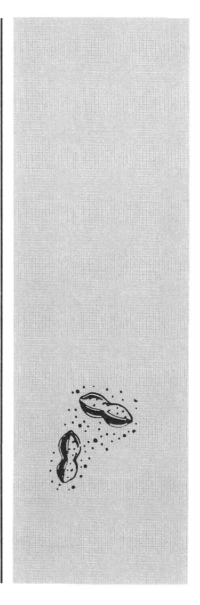

SIX

A Cook's Tour of Main Dishes with Peanut Butter

•■●■▲●■▲●■▲●■▲●■▲●■▲●■▲●■▲●■▲●■▲●■▲●■▲●

I used to get a lot of flak, but now
I'm as all-around popular as peanut butter.
—BETTE MIDLER, SINGER-ACTOR

By a 1974 decree of Congress, March is National Peanut Butter Month in the United States. In a country enamored of peanut butter, such an important event does not go unnoticed! The Senate restaurant, for example, serves a celebratory peanut butter dinner all during March. And every restaurant member of Chicago's Fine Dining Association offers a specially created peanut butter entrée on its menu.

Why not follow their lead—not just in March but throughout the year, whenever the timing seems right? Whether it's a family supper, a dinner for guests, a feast for a special occasion, or all three rolled into one, a main dish featuring peanut butter can be a delectable and much-appreciated change of pace. The recipes in this chapter help you give center stage to peanut butter and, in the process, to your own originality.

ROAST PORK WITH PEANUT BUTTER–HONEY MUSTARD GLAZE

•■▲●■▲●

SERVES 6–10

Roast Pork with Peanut Butter–Honey Mustard Glaze may sound down-home, but it's a dish fit for royalty. President Jimmy Carter,

Deglazing involves adding liquid to pan juices and then, over heat, scraping apart browned bits of food with a wooden spoon. This removes the natural glaze that has accumulated in the pan and creates a base for a natural or enriched sauce.

during his four-year break from peanut farming, served a variation of it to Queen Elizabeth and Prince Philip at a White House dinner. It offers a regal medley of tastes and textures, with the rich juiciness of the meat nicely counterbalanced by the savory-sweet tang of the glaze. As a bonus, it's easy to prepare and has a wonderful aroma, making it a perfect main course for a holiday dinner. Sliced paper thin, this recipe serves 10; sliced in slabs, 6.

3/4 cup dry red wine, divided
1/4 cup peanut butter
*1/4 cup honey mustard, at room
   temperature*
2 teaspoons crushed dried sage leaves

*4 1/2 pound boneless pork loin, center
   cut*
*4 garlic cloves, sliced in half
   lengthwise*

1. Preheat oven to 325°F.

2. To prepare glaze, combine 1/4 cup wine, peanut butter, mustard, and sage in small bowl. Remove 3 tablespoons of the mixture and set aside.

3. Place pork fat side up on roasting rack in pan. Make 4 slits in pork and push 2 garlic halves into each slit. Brush with half the remaining peanut butter mixture to coat.

4. Roast 3 to 3 1/2 hours, or until meat thermometer registers 160°F. Brush with remaining peanut butter mixture halfway through roasting. Let roast rest 15 minutes for easier carving.

5. To prepare gravy, add remaining wine and 1/2 cup water to roasting pan. Deglaze over medium heat for 5 minutes, stirring frequently. Remove from heat. Strain gravy into small saucepan. Whisk reserved 3 tablespoons peanut butter mixture into gravy over low heat.

6. Slice pork. Drizzle with warm gravy.

TURKEY-MOLASSES POT PIE
●■▲●■▲●
SERVES 6–8

The pot pie is a southern U.S. version of the age-old English "pasty" or meat pie, made bigger to accommodate the southern bounty of vegetables. In general, people regard pot pie as a satisfying comfort food. This particular pot pie is especially comforting, with its peanut-flavored crust and a hint of sweetness in the filling. Try it with leftover Thanksgiving turkey, instead of relying on the usual turkey sandwiches or turkey divan. For variations, replace the turkey with leftover chicken, pork, or beef; the other filling ingredients go well with all meats or poultry.

PASTRY

³/₄ cup all-purpose flour
¹/₂ cup stone-ground yellow cornmeal
¹/₂ teaspoon salt

¹/₃ cup chilled vegetable shortening
¹/₄ cup peanut butter
3–4 tablespoons ice water

FILLING

3 cups canned or fresh chicken broth
2 cups (about ³/₄ pound) red new potatoes, scrubbed and cut into 1-inch cubes
¹/₂ cup (2 medium) pared, diced carrots
¹/₂ cup (1 medium) chopped onion
¹/₂ cup fresh or thawed frozen peas
¹/₂ cup fresh or thawed frozen corn kernels

¹/₂ cup milk
¹/₃ cup peanut butter
2 tablespoons all-purpose flour
2 tablespoons stone-ground yellow cornmeal
2 tablespoons molasses
¹/₄ teaspoon freshly ground pepper
2 cups chopped cooked turkey

1. To prepare pastry, combine flour, cornmeal, and salt in large bowl. Cut in shortening and peanut butter with a pastry blender, until mixture resembles coarse crumbs. Sprinkle with ice water, 1 tablespoon at a time. Toss with a fork until dough forms. Flatten into disk and wrap in plastic wrap. Refrigerate 30 minutes.

2. In large dutch oven, bring broth to a boil over high heat. Add potatoes, carrots, and onion. Reduce heat to medium, cover, and cook 5 minutes. Add peas and corn. Cover and cook 5 minutes longer.

3. Preheat oven to 350°F.

4. In 2-cup measure, whisk next 6 ingredients until blended. Gradually add to simmering vegetable mixture. Stir frequently until mixture

is thick (about 10 minutes). Remove from heat. Stir in turkey. Spoon into 2-quart casserole. Set aside.

5. Between 2 sheets of plastic wrap, roll dough 1-inch larger than size of casserole. Remove 1 sheet. Invert dough on top of turkey mixture. Remove remaining sheet. Crimp edges to seal, and cut four 2-inch slits to allow steam to escape.

6. Bake 50–60 minutes, until browned. Let stand 10 minutes before serving.

REAL TEXAS CHILI

●■▲●■▲●

SERVES 6

What is "real" chili? It's perhaps the most hotly debated food question in the United States.

A dish similar to what the majority of Americans call chili existed in pre-Columbian Mexico. The early Spanish colonizers transplanted the large domesticated chilis necessary to make that dish from Mexico to Texas. In time, a San Antonio cook gave birth to the first recognizably American chili—or so the San Antonio Chamber of Commerce claims. But true Texas chili lovers don't even call the dish chili; they call it a "bowl of red."

I consider this chili "real" because it's based on the most essential and fundamentally delicious chili ingredients—including chunks of beef instead of chopped meat. To leave my own brand on the dish (after all, a chili-making tradition), I've added another ancient Mexican delight, peanut butter. In addition to making a great bowl of red, this chili can be served over rice with either flour or corn tortillas.

1/4 cup chili powder
2 tablespoons all-purpose flour
2 teaspoons ground cumin
2 tablespoons vegetable oil
2 pounds boneless beef chuck, trimmed of fat, cut into 1-inch pieces

2 garlic cloves, chopped
1 (13³/4-ounce) can beef broth
1/2 cup peanut butter
1 tablespoon dried oregano
1 teaspoon salt
2 (15-ounce) cans red kidney beans, rinsed and drained

1. On wax paper, combine first 3 ingredients. Dredge meat in mixture to coat (reserve remaining chili mixture).

2. In large dutch oven, heat oil over medium-high heat. Add beef and garlic. Sauté until browned on all sides (about 10 minutes).

3. In 4-cup measure, whisk broth, peanut butter, oregano, salt, reserved chili mixture, and 1 cup water until blended. Carefully pour over browned beef. Bring to boil. Reduce heat and simmer, partially covered, 1½ hours until meat is very tender, stirring occasionally. Add more water if necessary.

4. Stir in beans. Cook 15 minutes longer until heated through.

OVEN-BARBECUED RIBS

● ■ ▲ ● ■ ▲ ●

SERVES 6–8

For a barbecue meal anytime of the year, Oven-barbecued Ribs will help you blaze a new and crowd-pleasing trail. The sauce has a wonderful smoky-smooth peanut butter flavor that sets it well apart from routine barbecue sauces. It's also very versatile. Use it over any meat or poultry for a taste as fresh and as large as all outdoors.

6 pounds pork spareribs, cut in 1-rib widths

SAUCE (2 CUPS)

³/₄ cup catsup	*1 tablespoon molasses*
¹/₂ cup peanut butter	*1 tablespoon Worcestershire sauce*
¹/₄ cup finely chopped onion	*2 teaspoons paprika*
3 tablespoons fresh lemon juice	*¹/₂ teaspoon salt*
2 tablespoons vegetable oil	*¹/₄ teaspoon dry mustard*

1. To prepare barbecue sauce, whisk all ingredients in a 2-cup measure with ¹/₄ cup water until blended.

2. Arrange ribs in a single layer in large roasting pan. Brush ribs with sauce, using all of it. Cover with foil and refrigerate overnight.

3. Preheat oven to 350°F. Roast foil-covered ribs 45 minutes. Remove foil. Roast 45 minutes longer.

To grill instead of bake, cut ribs in pieces of 2–3 ribs. Brush ribs with half the sauce. Cover and refrigerate overnight. Place ribs on grill over medium-hot fire. Brush with half the remaining sauce. Close grill lid and cook 15 minutes. Turn ribs and brush with remaining sauce. Close grill lid and cook 15 minutes longer.

SOUTHWEST PIZZA

●■▲●■▲●

MAKES 1 12-INCH PIZZA

Julienne strips are about ⅛-inch thick and usually about 2 inches long, but the length may vary.

Contrary to popular myth, pizza is *not* an American creation. It's a traditional Italian dish, first introduced to the United States by nineteenth-century Neapolitans settling in New York City. The word *pizza* is widely believed to have come from the Italian verb *pizzacare*, or "to pluck," referring to the quick action required to get the hot flatbread pie out of the wood-burning oven.

This particular pizza may be Italian in heritage, but it's definitely American in flavor—specifically southwest American, with smoked chicken, goat cheese, sun-dried tomatoes, and, of course, peanut butter. It was inspired by a splendid southwestern pizza I ate at the Santacafe in Santa Fe, New Mexico. Like most good pizzas, this one is easy to make and it's simply mouth-watering.

DOUGH

½ cup warm water (105–115°F)
1 package active dry yeast
½ teaspoon sugar

1½ cups all-purpose flour
½ teaspoon salt
2 tablespoons peanut oil

TOPPING

⅓ cup peanut butter
2 tablespoons peanut oil, divided
1 tablespoon balsamic vinegar
½ teaspoon each, chili powder and ground cumin
2 ounces (about ½ cup) smoked chicken, cut into julienne strips
*2 ounces (about ½ cup) goat cheese, crumbled ***

½ cup sun-dried tomatoes (soaked in warm water, if necessary), chopped
¼ cup chopped fresh cilantro (coriander)
3 tablespoons thinly sliced scallion
2 tablespoons chopped, salted dry-roasted peanuts

1. To prepare dough, in food processor fitted with steel blade combine water, yeast, and sugar. Let stand 10 minutes until foamy. Add

flour and salt. Pulse 3–4 times to combine. With machine running, add oil. Process dough for 40 seconds to knead. On lightly floured surface, knead dough an additional 2–3 minutes, adding a little more flour if necessary.

2. Place dough in medium bowl brushed with oil. Turn to coat. Cover with clean towel or plastic wrap. Let rise in a warm, draft-free place until doubled in size (about 1 hour).

3. To prepare topping, combine peanut butter, 1 tablespoon oil, vinegar, chili powder, and cumin in small bowl. Set aside.

4. Preheat oven to 500°F. Lightly oil a 12-inch pizza pan. Punch down dough. Place in center of pan. With fingers, press dough to edges of pan.

5. Spread peanut butter mixture to within ½ inch of edge. Sprinkle remaining ingredients evenly over top. Drizzle with remaining oil.

6. Bake 12–15 minutes on bottom rack of oven until crisp and browned.

* Shredded Monterey Jack cheese may be substituted for goat cheese.

For a method of preparing the dough by hand, see the recipe for Peanut Butter–Olive Focaccia on page 35.

MAPLE–PEANUT BUTTER–GLAZED TURKEY WITH PEANUT-CORNBREAD STUFFING

●■▲●■▲●

SERVES 14–18

No, the turkey is not a Middle Eastern bird, despite its name. Nor is roast turkey anything but an all-American dish. However, roast turkey was almost certainly *not* served at the first Thanksgiving. Its link with Thanksgiving appears to have begun around the time that the United States formally came into being, when Benjamin Franklin was pushing the turkey, rather than the bald eagle, as a candidate for our national symbol. This recipe offers a refreshingly updated version of roast turkey, adding the decidedly American flavors of maple and peanut.

1 14-pound turkey

STUFFING *

¹/₂ cup (1 stick) unsalted butter
¹/₃ cup peanut butter
1 (1-pound) bag cornbread stuffing mix
1 medium apple, pared, cored, and chopped

¹/₃ cup chopped salted dry-roasted peanuts
¹/₄ cup chopped flat-leaf parsley
¹/₂ teaspoon salt
¹/₄ teaspoon freshly ground pepper

GLAZE

¹/₃ cup pure maple syrup
¹/₄ cup peanut butter

¹/₄ cup (¹/₂ stick) unsalted butter, cut into pieces

1. To prepare stuffing, combine butter, peanut butter, and 2¹/₂ cups water in medium saucepan. Cook over medium heat until butter is melted and mixture is smooth, stirring frequently.

2. In large bowl, combine remaining ingredients. Add butter mixture, tossing to coat. Set aside.

3. Preheat oven to 325°F.

4. To prepare glaze, combine maple syrup, butter, and peanut butter in small saucepan over medium heat. Stir occasionally until butter is melted and mixture is smooth.

5. Remove turkey giblets and neck from body cavity. Rinse turkey and pat dry with paper towels. Loosely fill body and neck cavity of turkey with stuffing. Skewer neck cavity shut. Truss the turkey with twine, tying legs together to close large cavity, or place in metal band. Place turkey, breast side up, on rack in roasting pan. Brush entire surface with ¹/₂ of the glaze. Roast, basting occasionally with pan juices and remaining glaze, about 4 hours or until meat thermometer inserted in the inner thigh reaches 185°F. If turkey browns too quickly, cover with foil tent. Let rest 15 minutes for easier carving.

* The stuffing may be used to stuff two 7–8-pound chickens instead of one 14-pound turkey. As a side dish with meat, place in a baking dish, cover with foil, and bake 1 hour.

BEEF WELLINGTON IN PUMPKIN BRIOCHE

●■▲●■▲●

SERVES 8

As far as experts can tell, beef Wellington (essentially a beef fillet encased in a pastry shell) hails from Ireland, where it was the favorite dish of the Irish-born Duke of Wellington, victor at Waterloo. Now it's a favorite dish in American homes and restaurants, such as the newly renovated Rainbow Room in New York City.

Beef Wellington in Pumpkin Brioche uses peanut butter in the dough (a brioche is a slightly sweet yeast bread) as well as in the duxelle filling (a duxelle is a paste made from finely chopped mushrooms and shallots). It's a very hearty dish that's especially good in the winter. I suggest serving it with very thin green beans sauteed in olive oil and butter, and a diced tomato salad with red onions, oregano, salt, and olive oil.

8 4–5-ounce beef tenderloins

BRIOCHE DOUGH

1 package active dry yeast
¼ cup warm water (105–115°F)
1 teaspoon sugar
2 cups all-purpose flour
½ teaspoon salt
½ teaspoon ground cloves

½ cup (1 stick) unsalted butter, chilled and cut into 8 pieces
½ cup canned or fresh pureed pumpkin
½ cup peanut butter
2 large eggs, at room temperature

DUXELLE FILLING

¼ cup (½ stick) unsalted butter, cut into 4 pieces
½ cup peanut oil, divided
1 pound mushrooms, minced
2 tablespoons minced shallots
½ teaspoon salt

2 tablespoons brandy
1 cup peanut butter
¼ cup all-purpose flour
1 teaspoon salt
½ teaspoon ground nutmeg

GLAZE

1 large egg, lightly beaten

1. To prepare brioche dough, combine yeast, water, and sugar in 2-cup measure. Set aside.

2. In food processor fitted with steel blade, combine flour, salt, and cloves. Pulse 5 times to combine. Add butter. Process 15 seconds.

3. In small saucepan, combine pumpkin and peanut butter. Stir over low heat until peanut butter melts (about 3 minutes). Remove from heat. Set aside.

4. Whisk eggs into yeast mixture. With food processor running, pour mixture through feed tube. Process 1 minute. Add peanut butter mixture. Process 30 seconds. Dough will be sticky.

5. Place dough in large oiled bowl. Cover with oiled plastic wrap. Let rise 2 hours or until almost tripled in size. Scrape dough down with a spatula. Cover and refrigerate overnight.

6. The next day, preheat oven to 425°F.

7. To prepare duxelle, in 12-inch skillet melt butter with ¼ cup oil over high heat. Add mushrooms, shallots, and salt. Sauté until mushroom liquid is absorbed (about 8–10 minutes), stirring frequently. Add brandy. Cook 2 minutes. Remove from heat. Vigorously stir in peanut butter until mixture is smooth. Place in bowl. Set aside.

8. On wax paper, combine flour, salt, and nutmeg. Dredge each tenderloin in mixture to coat.

9. In same skillet, heat remaining peanut oil over medium-high heat. Sear tenderloins on all sides (about 5 minutes). Remove from heat. Set aside.

10. Remove brioche from refrigerator. On lightly floured surface, divide dough into 8 equal pieces. Roll one piece at a time into 8 × 7-inch rectangle. Spread scant ¼ cup duxelle mixture over center. Place 1 tenderloin on top. Lift sides and ends of dough over top to close. Invert, and place on large, oiled baking sheet. Repeat with remaining dough, duxelle, and meat. Brush each with egg to glaze.

11. Bake 10 minutes. Reduce heat to 350°F and bake 10 minutes longer for medium rare.

AROMATIC INDIAN STEW

●■▲●■▲●

SERVES 6

The peanut arrived in India around 1670—just in time to delight and sustain the builders of the Taj Mahal. From that moment on, the peanut became a cherished part of Indian cuisine. With its distinctive taste and thickening properties, peanut butter lends itself especially well to traditional Indian stews.

This particular Indian stew offers an exceptionally hearty and fragrant example. I suggest serving it with brown rice, lentils, chapati bread, flour tortillas, or even pita bread. An accompanying bowl of minted yogurt will cool the palate.

2 (10-ounce) boxes frozen peas
3 tablespoons vegetable oil
1½ cups finely chopped onions
2 garlic cloves, minced
1 teaspoon finely chopped gingerroot
1 teaspoon ground cumin
1 teaspoon turmeric
½ teaspoon ground red pepper

1½ pounds ground lamb or lean beef
1 (28-ounce) can crushed tomatoes
¼ cup peanut butter
1 teaspoon salt
¼ cup chopped fresh cilantro (coriander)
*2 teaspoons garam masala ***

1. Remove peas from freezer. Let stand at room temperature.
2. In large dutch oven, heat oil over medium heat. Add onions and cook 20–25 minutes, stirring frequently, until browned.
3. Stir in garlic and ginger. Cook 2 minutes. Add cumin, turmeric, and pepper.
4. Stir in meat, breaking it up with a fork or wooden spoon. Cook until it loses its pink color (about 10 minutes).
5. Add tomatoes, peanut butter, and salt. Reduce heat and simmer, covered, 35 minutes, stirring occasionally.
6. Add peas (breaking up with fingers if still frozen), cilantro, and

* Garam masala is a combination of spices used in many Indian dishes. It is available at Indian markets. If not available, combine 1 teaspoon ground cardamom, ½ teaspoon ground cinnamon, and ¼ teaspoon each ground cumin, coriander, and black pepper.

garam masala. Cook 10–15 minutes, covered, until peas are heated through, stirring occasionally.

GRILLED SZECHUAN SHRIMP IN THEIR SHELLS

●■▲●■▲●

SERVES 4

No country in the world—including the United States—has taken to the peanut as wholeheartedly and creatively as China, particularly the central Szechuan region, which is famous for its spicy cuisine. In this recipe, the peanut's robust flavor enlivens a Szechuan-style dipping sauce for shrimp.

This dish is fabulous in the summertime: colorful to the eye and zesty to the palate. For an exotic midsummer night's dinner, I recommend serving it with a room-temperature rice salad that includes peas, the tomato pulp remaining from the recipe, golden raisins, and a vinaigrette dressing.

¹/₄ cup vegetable oil	*1 tablespoon chili paste**
5 tablespoons peanut butter	*8 jumbo (about 1¹/₂ pounds) shrimp,*
¹/₄ cup chopped fresh cilantro	*in their shells*
(coriander)	*4 medium tomatoes*
3 tablespoons rice wine vinegar*	
1¹/₂ tablespoons minced peeled	
gingerroot	

1. In large bowl, combine first 6 ingredients with ¹/₄ cup water until smooth. Remove ¹/₂ cup of the mixture. Set aside. Add shrimp to bowl. Toss to coat. Let stand 30 minutes at room temperature, stirring occasionally.

2. Prepare grill according to manufacturer's instructions.

3. Slice off tops of tomatoes. Discard. With spoon, scoop out tomato pulp (reserve for other recipes). Place tomatoes cut-side down on paper towels to drain for 15 minutes. Spoon about 2 tablespoons remaining peanut sauce into each tomato shell. Set aside.

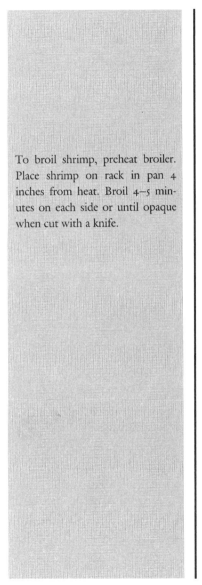

To broil shrimp, preheat broiler. Place shrimp on rack in pan 4 inches from heat. Broil 4–5 minutes on each side or until opaque when cut with a knife.

4. Grill shrimp 4 inches from hot coals 4–5 minutes on each side or until opaque when cut with a knife. Place 2 shrimp and 1 tomato shell with dipping sauce on each serving plate.

* Rice vinegar and chili paste are available at Asian markets.

SENEGALESE GROUNDNUT STEW
●■▲●■▲●
SERVES 4–6

Senegal is the French name for a former colony, and groundnut is the word most commonly used by the English for peanut (because it grows along or below the ground). Nevertheless, Senegalese Groundnut Stew is pure African.

All across Africa, the dietary mainstay is a stew accompanied by a starchy food. The nature of the starchy food varies according to region. In North Africa, for example, it tends to be couscous, a pebbly-fine cereal. In other areas it may be corn, rice, yams, or even bananas. As for the stew part of the meal, it consists of whatever happens to be available, but in equatorial central and West Africa, it *always* includes peanuts and red pepper. Try this flavorful version of a typical Senagalese stew on rice, couscous, or orzo.

¹/₄ cup peanut oil
1 3-pound chicken, cut into 16 pieces
1 large onion (about ¹/₂ pound), chopped
1 teaspoon minced, peeled gingerroot
4 ripe plum tomatoes (about ¹/₂ pound), chopped
2 sweet potatoes (about 1¹/₂ pounds), pared and coarsely chopped
3 parsnips (about ³/₄ pound), pared and chopped

4 turnips (about 1 pound), pared and chopped
³/₄ cup old-fashioned-style peanut butter
2 cups okra (about ¹/₂ pound), washed, trimmed, and coarsely sliced
³/₄ teaspoon salt
¹/₂ teaspoon ground red pepper

1. In large dutch oven, heat oil over medium-high heat. Add chicken pieces, turning until browned on all sides (about 5 minutes). Remove with slotted spoon. Drain on paper towels and set aside.

2. Add onion and gingerroot to pot. Cook 2–3 minutes until soft. Stir in vegetables (except okra), then place chicken pieces on top. Pour in 4 cups water. Bring to a boil. Reduce heat and simmer, covered, 30 minutes, until vegetables are tender.

3. In 2-cup measure, whisk peanut butter with 1 cup broth from pot. Stir into stew with okra, salt, and pepper. Simmer, uncovered, over medium heat 15 minutes longer, stirring frequently.

GRILLED SCALLOPS ON
CURRIED PEANUT FRIED RICE

●■▲●■▲●

SERVES 3–4

The taste of curry epitomizes Indian cuisine. Typically, cooks in India grind their own fresh curry daily. They draw from a variety of spices, herbs, and seeds, according to product availability and their own day-to-day whim. Among the most prevalent ingredients are cardamom, cinnamon, cloves, coriander, cumin, fennel seed, mace, pepper, nutmeg, saffron, tamarind, and turmeric; but the ultimate curry might easily include up to 20 different components.

Most commercial curry powders are significantly blander than their authentic home-ground Indian counterparts. I like a relatively hot curry, which is why I recommend Madras curry powder (the hot commercial variety) for this recipe. If you prefer a mild curry, by all means use regular curry powder. Either way, this dish has a great spicy, peanutty flavor, as well as a beautiful orange-red color.

1 pound sea scallops
2 tablespoons peanut oil

¹/₂ teaspoon five-spice powder *

SAUCE

¹/₂ cup chopped red bell pepper
¹/₄ cup chunky-style peanut butter

1 tablespoon soy sauce
1 garlic clove

FRIED RICE

3 tablespoons peanut oil
1 cup sliced scallion, white and green
* parts*
2 teaspoons Madras curry powder

4 cups cooked rice
Sliced green scallion to garnish

1. In 8-inch baking pan, combine scallops, oil, and five-spice powder. Set aside.

2. To prepare sauce, combine all ingredients with ¼ cup water in blender. Process until smooth and set aside.

3. Preheat broiler.

4. To prepare rice, heat oil in large skillet over medium-high heat. Sauté scallions 2 minutes. Add curry powder. Stir 10 seconds. Add rice, stirring to break up. Pour sauce over mixture. Stir to combine. Reduce heat to low.

5. Place scallops in pan on broiler rack 4 inches from heat. Broil 8–10 minutes until opaque. Spoon onto rice in skillet. Garnish with scallion and serve immediately.

* Five-spice powder is available in Asian markets and some supermarkets.

THAI DUCK BREASTS
WITH LEMONGRASS
●■▲●■▲●
SERVES 4

Thais are fond of dishes that offer a complexity of taste tones—sweet and sour, hot and cold, strong and subtle. Peanuts and lemongrass, both of which grow well in the tropical climate of Thailand, have a chameleonlike ability to blend with a wide spectrum of ingredients, while still retaining their distinctive characters. Inevitably, they became primary elements of Thai cooking.

Thai Duck Breasts with Lemongrass offers a spectacular medley of flavors with citric overtones. It's so popular with diners that I recommend cooking 6 breasts to serve 4 people: 1 breast per person (each

breast shrinks to half-size when cooked), with 2 in reserve. Leftover duck, if any, can be incorporated into a future meal by slicing the duck thinly and using the slices in a salad with a honey dressing.

To accompany Thai Duck Breasts with Lemongrass, I suggest steamed snow peas mixed with straw mushrooms (drained from the can) and Chinese noodles seasoned with dark sesame oil. Serve with a chilled gewurtztraminer (an Alsatian wine).

2 stalks fresh lemongrass
2 tablespoons fresh cilantro (coriander)
1 tablespoon minced, peeled gingerroot
2 garlic cloves
2 (1½-inch) dried hot red chilis **
¼ cup (2 large limes) fresh lime juice

¼ cup old-fashioned-style peanut butter
2 tablespoons rice wine vinegar
2 tablespoons peanut oil
1 teaspoon coarse salt
3 whole boneless duck breasts, split in half

1. Trim lemongrass. Discard outer leaves. Cut stalk, leaving bottom bulb plus 1 inch of stalk. Slice thinly.

2. In food processor fitted with steel blade, combine lemongrass, cilantro, gingerroot, garlic, and chilis. Process 40 seconds until minced. Add lime juice, peanut butter, vinegar, oil, and salt. Process 30 seconds until smooth.

3. Place duck breasts, skin side up, on rack in roasting pan. Brush both sides of breast with marinade, using all the marinade. Refrigerate, covered with plastic wrap, for 3 hours.

4. Preheat oven to 450°F.

5. Remove plastic wrap from pan. Place in oven. Roast breasts 15 minutes. Reduce heat to 300°F and roast 10 minutes longer for medium done. Serve immediately.

* Dried hot red chilis are available in Asian markets.

PEANUT-CRUSTED MAHIMAHI

●■▲●■▲●

SERVES 4

The peanut converged on Polynesia from three directions during the eighteenth and nineteenth centuries: northwest from China, southwest from Indonesia, and northeast from North, Central, and South America. Indeed, Polynesia can be considered the final frontier of the peanut (although U.S. astronauts have lately been taking peanut butter into outer space).

By contrast, Polynesia has long revered the native dorado or "dolphin" fish (not a true dolphin, or even a mammal). Called mahimahi by the Hawaiians, it's a firmly textured fish—like swordfish—with a very appealing sweet but full-bodied taste. In this recipe, that taste is deliciously enhanced by peanuttiness. Serve Peanut-crusted Mahimahi with cilantro-topped, grilled tomato slices and garlic bread. For a good wine accompaniment, try a chilled '83 spatlese (a German wine).

¹/₂ cup pineapple juice
¹/₄ cup soy sauce
2 tablespoons old-fashioned-style peanut butter
1 tablespoon dark brown sugar
¹/₂ teaspoon five-spice powder*
4 6-ounce mahimahi fillets, skin removed, or swordfish steaks

¹/₂ cup cornstarch (sift if lumpy)
3 tablespoons finely chopped unsalted dry-roasted peanuts
¹/₄ cup peanut oil
1 cup chopped very ripe mango to garnish (optional)

1. To prepare marinade, whisk first 5 ingredients in 2-cup measure until blended.

2. Place fillets in shallow dish. Pour marinade over fish to cover. Let stand 2 hours, turning occasionally, or refrigerate, covered, up to 4 hours.

3. On wax paper, combine cornstarch and peanuts. Dredge each fillet in the mixture, pressing coating onto both sides.

4. In 12-inch skillet, heat oil over medium-high heat. Add fish and cook 3–4 minutes on each side until browned. Garnish with mango if desired.

* Five-spice powder is available in Asian markets.

SEVEN

Out-of-This-World Peanut Butter Snacks & Desserts

●■▲●■▲●■▲●■▲●■▲●■▲●■▲●■▲●■▲●■▲●■▲●■▲●■▲●■▲●

No matter how stuffed I get,
there's always room for peanut butter.
—DINAH SHORE,
SINGER AND TELEVISION HOST

The English refer to every proper meal as going "from soup to nuts." Their point is well taken. Nuts and nut flavors give extra-special substance and satisfaction to dessert and, for that matter, to dessertlike treats at any time of the day.

Peanut butter, especially, is in its natural element when it comes to snacks and desserts. It all began long before there was an England, when the ancient natives of Central America and Mexico ground peanuts with honey as a delicacy for festive occasions. Since that time, peanuts have been used to flavor sweets, puddings, candies, and assorted baked goods throughout Africa, Asia, and, ultimately, the United States. George Washington Carver's famous 1925 peanut cookbook offered recipes for 41 different peanut butter snacks and desserts, many of them based on traditional dishes in African-American, Native American, or European-American cooking.

In contemporary America, by far the most well-known and often-eaten peanut butter treat is the peanut butter cookie. Although the peanut butter cookie remains a good home base for a dessert or a snack, it's high time for cooks to go forth boldly into the unknown. Use the peanut butter recipes in this chapter to reach new, spectacular worlds of dessert and snack pleasure!

OLD-FASHIONED NUTTY
PEANUT BUTTER COOKIES

●■▲●■▲●

MAKES 4½ DOZEN COOKIES

During the World War II years, American enthusiasm for peanut butter as an economical and delicious foodstuff ran high. It inspired home-front bakers to create a uniquely patriotic, easy-to-prepare, and deliciously reassuring treat: the peanut butter cookie. This book would not be complete without its own bigger and better peanut butter cookie recipe.

Old-fashioned Nutty Peanut Butter Cookies have extra peanut chunks and one fourth more peanut butter than most other recipes allow. They may be old-fashioned in appeal, but they're crisply brand-new in taste.

1½ cups all-purpose flour
1½ teaspoons baking powder
Pinch of salt
6 tablespoons unsalted butter, cut in pieces

¾ cup packed dark brown sugar
¾ cup peanut butter
1 large egg, lightly beaten
½ cup coarsely chopped salted dry-roasted peanuts

1. Preheat oven to 375°F. Coat 2 baking sheets with vegetable oil cooking spray, and set aside.

2. In medium bowl, combine first 3 ingredients.

3. In large bowl of electric mixer, cream butter at medium speed until light and fluffy. Add sugar. Beat 3–5 minutes. Add peanut butter and egg, beating until blended, scraping down sides of bowl.

4. At low speed, add flour mixture gradually. Fold in nuts.

5. Roll mixture into 1-inch balls. Place 2 inches apart on prepared baking sheets. Press down on each cookie with tines of fork, making a criss-cross.

6. Bake about 10 minutes, or until lightly brown around edges. Turn onto rack to cool. Store in airtight container.

PEANUT BUTTER–MINT
MERINGUE COOKIES
●■▲●■▲●
MAKES 24 COOKIES

Did you ever put a dab of peanut butter on a chocolate-covered mint? Wasn't it sinfully good? This recipe provides an even more delectable rendition of that taste combination, in a melt-in-your-mouth meringue form. The astronaut Alan Shepard took a peanut to the moon. Now let Peanut Butter–Mint Meringue Cookies take you to heaven.

3 large egg whites at room
   temperature
1/8 teaspoon cream of tartar
1/2 cup sugar

1/2 cup chunky-style peanut butter
1/4 cup water
*1/2 cup mint-flavored chocolate chips **

1. Preheat oven to 275°F. Coat 2 baking sheets with vegetable oil cooking spray. Set aside.

2. In small bowl of electric mixer, beat egg whites at medium speed until frothy. Add cream of tartar and beat at medium speed. Gradually add sugar and beat until mixture is stiff and glossy but not dry.

3. In medium bowl, combine peanut butter and water. Fold in 1/3 egg white mixture until well blended. Fold in remaining egg whites until combined. Add chips.

4. Drop heaping tablespoonfuls onto prepared pan. Bake 40–45 minutes. Let cool in pan on wire rack for 10 minutes. Remove with a spatula.

* Peanut butter chips, chocolate chips, or any combination of chips may be substituted.

For best results, bake these cookies on layered baking sheets. Cushionaire is the brand name of a widely available product. A layered baking sheet is insulated and therefore distributes the heat more evenly.

CHOCOLATE "LACED" COOKIES

●■▲●■▲●

MAKES 36 SANDWICH COOKIES

This is no ordinary lace cookie but a festive "laced" cookie. Based on a traditional southern Christmas treat, Chocolate "Laced" Cookies are even more southern in character, thanks to the addition of peanut butter. In keeping with the fanciness of the sandwich cookie itself, the baking process is fairly intricate. You may want to turn that process into a two-person operation to add to the festivities.

³/₄ cup rolled oats
¹/₂ cup packed dark brown sugar
¹/₂ cup finely chopped salted dry-
  roasted peanuts

2 tablespoons all-purpose flour
7 tablespoons unsalted butter, melted
2 tablespoons dark corn syrup
1 teaspoon vanilla extract

FILLING

¹/₂ cup peanut butter

¹/₂ cup seedless red raspberry preserves

CHOCOLATE DRIZZLE

¹/₂ cup semisweet chocolate chips

1. Preheat oven to 350°F.
2. In large bowl, combine first 4 ingredients. In 1-cup measure, combine butter, corn syrup, and vanilla. Add liquid ingredients to dry until blended.
3. Spoon batter by ¹/₂ teaspoonfuls onto baking sheet, 4 inches apart. Bake 8–10 minutes, until golden brown. Let stand about 1 minute. With spatula, carefully remove cookies to wire rack to cool. (If cookies harden and stick to pan, place in oven again to soften.)
4. Place cooled cookies, flat side up, on lengths of wax paper. Lightly spread half the batch with peanut butter, and the other half with preserves. Sandwich each peanut butter side with a preserves side. Leave them on wax paper.
5. In small saucepan, melt chocolate over low heat, stirring constantly. Spoon chocolate into pastry bag fitted with a #4 tip (very

small hole). Drizzle chocolate in thin lines across cookies. Let stand 30 minutes. Store between sheets of wax paper in airtight container.

FROSTED PEANUT BUTTER BARS

●■▲●■▲●

MAKES 12 BARS

Frosted Peanut Butter Bars are a singularly tasty and healthy alternative to brownies. They're chewy, with a zesty orange flavor that's nicely duplicated in the creamy frosting. Like brownies, they serve equally well as a snack or a dessert, but unlike most brownies, they're also sufficiently hearty to make a novel and engaging breakfast treat.

3/4 cup packed light brown sugar
6 tablespoons unsalted butter, cut
 into pieces
*1/2 cup peanut butter ***
1 large egg

2 tablespoons orange juice
1 cup all-purpose flour
1 cup rolled oats
1/2 teaspoon baking soda
1/4 teaspoon salt

FROSTING

3/4 cup confectioners' sugar
*1/3 cup peanut butter ***
2 tablespoons orange juice

Pinch of salt
2 tablespoons chopped salted dry-
 roasted peanuts to garnish

1. Preheat oven to 350°F. Coat a 9-inch square baking pan with vegetable oil cooking spray. Set aside.

2. In large bowl of electric mixture, beat first 5 ingredients at medium speed until smooth and creamy, about five minutes.

3. In medium bowl, combine flour, oats, baking soda, and salt. Gradually add to peanut butter mixture, with machine running at low speed. Beat about 1 minute, until blended.

4. Spread batter into prepared pan. Bake about 20 minutes, or until a toothpick inserted into center comes out clean. Cool completely in pan on rack.

5. To prepare frosting, whisk sugar, peanut butter, orange juice, and salt in small bowl until smooth. Spread frosting evenly with spatula. Cut in half. Cut each *half* into 6 bars. Sprinkle with nuts.

* Do not use old-fashioned-style peanut butter or the bars will be too grainy.

AUNT ALICE FROM
DALLAS (OREGON) COOKIES
●■▲●■▲●

MAKES 36 COOKIES

These cookies are very easy to make and very hard to resist. They are also very original. Aunt Alice is the inventive great-aunt of Kathryn Cronin, who is now in training to swim the English Channel. May her great-aunt's chewy peanut butter delights channel some of her energy and sense of adventure to you!

1 cup peanut butter
1 cup sugar
1 large egg, lightly beaten

1 teaspoon vanilla extract
Pinch of salt

1. Preheat oven to 350°F.
2. In large bowl of electric mixer, beat all ingredients at medium speed 1 minute, until blended. Batter will be stiff.
3. Shape heaping teaspoonfuls into balls. Place on ungreased baking sheets. Press balls with back of fork to flatten.
4. Bake 12 minutes, or until lightly browned around edges. Cool on rack in pan 5 minutes. Remove with spatula and cool completely. Store in airtight container.

BLOWOUT BROWNIES
●■▲●■▲●

MAKES 20 BROWNIES

This is truly a megadessert, with marshmallows, peanut butter, and chocolate combined and primed to send you into orbit! For a party, you can cut down the individual brownie size to as small as a 1½-inch square and serve the brownies perched atop a doily on a footed silver tray. Even *that* tiny, Blowout Brownies still pack a major taste wallop!

2 cups sugar	*4 large eggs*
¾ cup (1½ sticks) unsalted butter, cut into pieces	*1½ teaspoons vanilla extract*
¾ cup chunky-style peanut butter	*1½ cups all-purpose flour*
6 (1-ounce) squares unsweetened chocolate, cut in half	*¼ teaspoon salt*
	1 cup peanut butter chips
	2 cups miniature marshmallows

CHOCOLATE DRIZZLE

¼ cup light corn syrup	*1½ tablespoons unsalted butter*
1½ (1-ounce) squares unsweetened chocolate	*Pinch of salt*

1. Coat 15 × 10 × 1-inch jelly roll pan with vegetable oil cooking spray. Set aside.

2. In heavy, medium saucepan, combine sugar, butter, peanut butter, and chocolate. Stir frequently over low heat, until chocolate melts and mixture begins to simmer (about 15 minutes). Remove from heat. Cool to lukewarm.

3. Preheat oven to 350°F.

4. In large bowl, whisk eggs and vanilla until combined. Add peanut butter mixture and whisk until blended. Gradually add flour and salt. Fold in chips.

5. Pour mixture into prepared pan. Spread evenly. Bake 18–20 minutes, or until a toothpick inserted into center comes out clean. Place pan on wire rack. Top with marshmallows immediately, pressing down until they begin to melt and stick.

6. To prepare chocolate drizzle, combine all ingredients in small saucepan. Stir constantly over low heat until well blended. Cool slightly. Drizzle over brownies in zigzag pattern. Let stand 1 hour. Cut into 3 × 2½-inch pieces and serve.

If you're in a hurry, add a couple of tablespoons of the hot chocolate mixture to the eggs, whisking constantly. Add a few more tablespoons until blended. This will raise the temperature of the eggs so the rest of the chocolate mixture can be incorporated without curdling the eggs. This is called tempering.

PEANUT BUTTER PIE

●■▲●■▲●

SERVES 10–12

Chill bowl and beaters for better volume.

Peanut Butter Pie is a wondrously gratifying dessert that is gaining more and more fans throughout the United States, thanks in part to the current trend toward country and new American cooking. This particular version is an adaptation of a recipe used at The Dimmick Inn in Milford, Pennsylvania. The cream cheese nicely balances the hearty peanut butter taste and adds its own slightly tangy richness.

PASTRY

$1^1/2$ cups graham cracker crumbs (about 16 graham cracker squares)

2 tablespoons sugar
$^1/2$ cup (1 stick) unsalted butter, melted and cooled

FILLING

$1^1/2$ cups heavy cream
12 ounces cream cheese, cut in chunks, at room temperature

1 cup peanut butter
$^3/4$ cup superfine sugar
2 teaspoons vanilla extract

TOPPING

$^3/4$ cup semisweet chocolate chips
1 tablespoon unsalted butter

2 tablespoons brewed coffee

1. To prepare crust, combine all ingredients in medium bowl. Press into a 9-inch pie pan or springform pan and freeze 1 hour.

2. To prepare filling, in small bowl of electric mixer beat cream at high speed until stiff beads form; set aside. Beat cream cheese, peanut butter, sugar, and vanilla in large bowl of electric mixer, using same beaters, until light and fluffy.

3. Fold half of the whipped cream into peanut butter mixture until combined. Repeat with remaining cream. Spoon mixture into frozen crust, spreading evenly. Cover lightly with foil. Refrigerate at least 6 hours.

4. To prepare topping, combine all ingredients in small saucepan. Stir constantly over low heat until chocolate and butter melt. Cool 15 minutes. Spread over pie to within 1 inch of rim. Refrigerate 1 hour.

BITTERSWEET CHOCOLATE–PEANUT LAYER CAKE

●■▲●■▲●

SERVES 10–12

The Bittersweet Chocolate–Peanut Layer Cake is truly magical. Not only is it extraordinarily delicious but it can also transform itself simply through refrigeration. Unrefrigerated, it consists of a cake layer and a peanut butter layer with a thick, shiny glaze of bittersweet chocolate. When refrigerated, the glaze solidifies, giving the cake a pleasingly different taste and texture. It's a thick, rich cake that's ideal for a mixed gathering of children and adults, especially when the occasion is a birthday. Just be sure to make enough so that you can enjoy it both ways!

CAKE

8 ounces bittersweet chocolate, chopped

1/2 cup (1 stick) unsalted butter, cut into pieces

3/4 cup sugar

3 large eggs lightly beaten, at room temperature

1/2 cup all-purpose flour

1/3 cup finely chopped salted dry-roasted peanuts

GLAZE

6 ounces bittersweet chocolate, chopped

1/4 cup (1/2 stick) unsalted butter, cut into pieces

1 tablespoon light corn syrup

1/2 cup heavy cream

Chopped salted peanuts to garnish (optional)

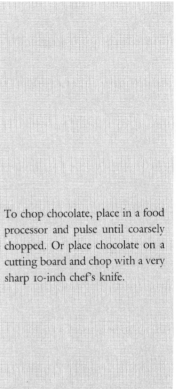

To chop chocolate, place in a food processor and pulse until coarsely chopped. Or place chocolate on a cutting board and chop with a very sharp 10-inch chef's knife.

TOPPING

³/₄ cup peanut butter *   *¹/₂ cup water*

1. Preheat oven to 350°F. Butter 9-inch round baking pan. Line with buttered parchment paper and set aside.

2. To prepare cake, in a double boiler over simmering water, melt chocolate and butter, stirring occasionally. Add sugar. Stir frequently until well blended, about 5 minutes. Remove from heat. Cool, stirring occasionally.

3. Whisk in eggs one at a time, beating well after each addition.

4. Fold in flour and peanuts until combined.

5. Spread batter evenly into pan. Bake 30–35 minutes, or until a toothpick inserted in center comes out clean. Cool on wire rack 30 minutes. Place a long sheet of wax paper under rack. Run knife around edge of pan and carefully invert cake onto rack. Peel off parchment paper.

6. To prepare glaze, combine all ingredients in medium saucepan over low heat, stirring occasionally until chocolate and butter are melted. Cool 10 minutes.

7. To prepare topping, in medium bowl combine peanut butter and water. Spread evenly over top of cake to form layer.

8. Pour glaze over cake. Let stand 15 minutes. With spatula, lift excess chocolate that has fallen through rack and spread onto cake evenly again. Repeat procedure until all of the glaze is used. If desired, press chopped peanuts around rim of cake.

* Don't use old-fashioned-style peanut butter in this recipe or the topping will not have a properly creamy consistency.

HONEY, VANILLA, AND PEANUT BUTTER
CHUNK ICE CREAM

● ■ ▲ ● ■ ▲ ●

MAKES 2 QUARTS

Ice cream has a remarkable traveling history. The practice of making a frozen dessert out of milk was unknown in the Western world until the thirteenth century, when Marco Polo brought back a recipe from Cathay (or China) to his native Venice. Ice cream mania quickly spread throughout Europe, and the subsequent Age of Exploration carried it everywhere that cows come home. As a result, ice cream has long been one of the most well-liked desserts on the globe. Explore new ice cream territory yourself with this novel and scrumptious blend.

2 cups half-and-half	*2 cups heavy cream*
2/3 cup honey	*1 tablespoon vanilla extract*
4 large egg yolks	*1 cup peanut butter* *

1. Whisk half-and-half, honey, and egg yolks in heavy, medium saucepan until blended. Cook over low heat until mixture thickens and coats the back of a spoon (about 30 minutes). Whisk frequently. Cool 30 minutes. Add cream and vanilla. Refrigerate, covered, at least 3 hours or overnight.

2. Pour mixture into container of ice cream machine. Process, following manufacturer's instructions. When ice cream is just about ready, turn off machine. Add peanut butter to mixture. Process 30 seconds. Remove dasher. Stir peanut butter into mixture with a pair of chopsticks or 2 knives.

3. Spoon mixture into a freezer container. Cover with plastic wrap and lid. Freeze overnight.

* Creamy-style peanut butter is preferable. Old-fashioned-style peanut butter disperses in ice cream, which prevents chunk formation and gives the ice cream a less attractive color.

Peanut butter tends to freeze when combined with ice cream. This may cause overly large chunks that need to be broken up. Chopsticks seem to be the most effective device for distributing peanut butter through ice cream, although the process is a bit messy.

Ice cream needs to be frozen overnight so that it can "ripen" to the proper consistency with full, even flavor distribution.

BANANA CHIP ICE CREAM

MAKES 1½ QUARTS

For generations, sandwich lovers have relished the combination of peanut butter and banana slices: a temperate, nutmeat heartiness enlivened by a tropical fruitiness. That combination is all the more enticing in a cold and creamy format, especially during the summertime. If you have any doubts, chill out with Banana Chip Ice Cream on a hot August evening.

2 teaspoons cornstarch
2 (12-ounce) cans evaporated milk
1 cup sugar
½ cup old-fashioned-style peanut butter

2 medium bananas
2 teaspoons fresh lemon juice
1 teaspoon vanilla extract
Pinch of salt
¼ cup mini chocolate chips

1. In small bowl, whisk cornstarch with 2 tablespoons evaporated milk. Add to medium saucepan with remaining milk and sugar. Cook over low heat 5 minutes, whisking frequently. Add peanut butter. Cook 5 minutes longer, whisking frequently until mixture is blended. Cool mixture 30 minutes. Refrigerate, covered, 1 hour.

2. On a plate, mash bananas. Sprinkle with lemon juice.

3. Add banana, vanilla, and salt to chilled mixture. Pour into container of ice cream machine. Process, following manufacturer's instructions. When ice cream is just about ready, add chips. Process until chips are distributed.

4. Spoon mixture into a freezer container. Cover with plastic wrap and lid. Freeze overnight.

PEANUT BUTTER CUSTARD
WITH SUGAR-GLAZED PEANUTS
●■▲●■●
SERVES 6

This recipe was inspired first by my love for French crème brulée, then by Bradley Ogden, one of my favorite American chefs, co-owner and executive chef of the Lark Creek Inn in Larkspur, California. The sugar-glazed peanuts can stand by themselves as peanut brittle (1 cup here), which gives you some idea of the rich, overall flavor of this melt-in-your-mouth treat. Serve the custard warm. It's also good cold, but keep in mind that it gets very thick during refrigeration because of the peanut butter.

SUGAR-GLAZED PEANUTS

1 tablespoon unsalted butter　　　　*3 tablespoons sugar*
1/2 cup salted dry-roasted peanuts

CUSTARD

4 egg yolks　　　　　　　　　　*1/8 teaspoon ground ginger*
1/4 cup peanut butter　　　　　　*1 cup heavy cream*
3 tablespoons sugar　　　　　　　*1 cup half-and-half*
1/2 teaspoon vanilla extract

1. Coat baking sheet with vegetable oil cooking spray. Set aside.

2. To prepare glazed peanuts, melt butter in small nonstick skillet over medium heat. Stir in peanuts to coat. Add sugar. Cook mixture until the sugar turns a golden amber in color (4–5 minutes), stirring frequently. Scrape mixture onto prepared pan. Cool until firm, then break into small pieces.

3. Preheat oven to 300°F. Place six 1/2-cup ramekins in a roasting pan. Set aside.

4. In blender, process first 5 custard ingredients until smooth. Set aside.

5. In heavy, medium saucepan, combine heavy cream and half-and-

half. Cook over medium-low heat just to boiling point. Remove saucepan from heat. Stir 2 tablespoons peanut butter mixture into cream. Pour mixture into blender. Blend to combine. Strain mixture through a sieve back into saucepan. Whisk constantly over low heat until mixture thickens, slightly coating back of a spoon (about 5 minutes).

6. Divide custard evenly among ramekins. Place roasting pan on oven rack. Pour hot water into pan to reach halfway up sides of ramekins. Bake about 35 minutes, until crust forms and is slightly jiggly in center. Top with glazed peanuts and serve immediately.

POACHED PEARS IN PEANUT BUTTER–CARAMEL SAUCE

●■▲●■▲●

SERVES 8

Poached Pears in Peanut Butter–Caramel Sauce are sweet, thick dinner-party fare that will honor your guests and leave them with a delightfully warm and fruity taste in their mouths, much like the taste of a soft, rosy wine.

Poaching fruit in general requires covering the fruit with water and then gently cooking it to just below the boiling point. Often poached fruit is served cold in its poaching syrup, without a sauce. In that case, Julia Child recommends adding 1½ cups of sugar to every quart of water in the syrup. You could try this approach using the syrup I describe here, but you'll miss the full peanut-buttery effect of the sauce.

8 slightly underripe Bartlett or Bosc pears
8 cups water

⅓ cup sugar
1 tablespoon fresh lemon juice

PEANUT BUTTER–CARAMEL SAUCE

½ cup sugar
½ cup half-and-half
¼ cup light corn syrup

Pinch of salt
¼ cup peanut butter *
3 tablespoons unsalted butter

1. Core pears from bottom, leaving stems intact. Peel.

2. In 4-quart saucepan, bring water, sugar, and lemon juice to a boil over high heat. Reduce heat. Add pears and simmer, covered, about 15 minutes, or until fork tender. Cool in liquid 30 minutes.**

3. To prepare sauce, in medium, heavy saucepan whisk first 4 ingredients over medium heat until combined. Bring to a boil, whisking frequently. Remove from heat. Whisk peanut butter and butter into mixture until smooth. Cover and keep warm.

4. Place pears on individual serving plates. Divide sauce evenly over each. Sauce will glaze pear and form a puddle around it.

* Do not use old-fashioned-style peanut butter or the sauce will be too grainy.
** To prepare ahead, cool pears in liquid. Cover with plastic wrap and refrigerate up to 4 hours. Bring to room temperature. Drain and pat dry with paper towels before spooning warm sauce over each.

PEANUTTY FUDGE SAUCE

●■▲●■▲●

MAKES 1½ CUPS

It is said that fudge began as a faddish homemade treat at New England women's colleges around the turn of the century. In fact, early varieties of fudge were named for different colleges, such as Wellesley fudge and Vassar fudge. Whatever the case, it was a New England woman, Sarah Dow, who invented hot fudge sauce, introducing it in 1906 at Bailey's, the famous Boston ice cream parlor.

Now a Brooklyn woman brings you Peanutty Fudge Sauce! Spoon it over ice cream, frozen yogurt, pound cake, or fruit for a divine taste sensation that's an education in itself.

2 (1-ounce) squares unsweetened
   chocolate, chopped
2 tablespoons unsalted butter
½ cup light corn syrup
¼ cup chunky-style peanut butter

¼ cup confectioners' sugar
¼ cup heavy cream
1 teaspoon vanilla extract
Pinch of salt

To chop chocolate, place in a small food processor and pulse until coarsely chopped. Or place chocolate on a cutting board and chop with a very sharp 10-inch chef's knife.

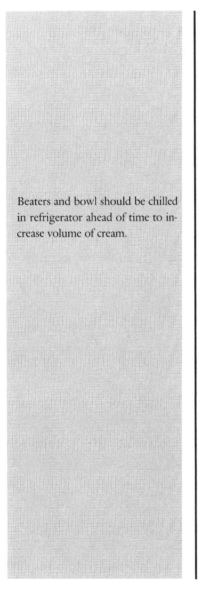

Beaters and bowl should be chilled in refrigerator ahead of time to increase volume of cream.

1. In small saucepan, combine chocolate and butter. Stir over medium heat until melted and blended.

2. Add remaining ingredients. Bring mixture to a boil. Reduce heat and simmer 3 minutes, stirring occasionally.

3. Serve warm. Refrigerate unused portion. To reheat, place in double boiler over simmering water.

PEANUT-MOCHA WHIPPED CREAM
●■▲●■▲●
MAKES 1¼ CUPS

Whipped cream is sumptuous all by itself. Peanut-Mocha Whipped Cream is ultrasumptuous and yet subtle enough in taste to blend delightfully with any kind of pudding, ice cream, or sherbet. For an elegant southern treat, use it as a topping on hot or iced bourbon-spiked coffee. If desired, this recipe can be halved.

3 tablespoons peanut butter
2 tablespoons strong brewed coffee, cold
½ teaspoon vanilla extract
1 cup chilled heavy cream
3 tablespoons confectioners' sugar

In small bowl of electric mixer, beat peanut butter, coffee, and vanilla at medium speed until smooth. With mixer running, pour in cream. Beat until soft peaks form. Increase speed to high. Gradually add sugar until cream is desired consistency. Be careful not to overbeat.

PEANUT-BUTTERY PRALINES
●■▲●■▲●
MAKES ABOUT 30 PRALINES

The luxuriously sweet confection known as a praline evokes romantic images of Creole New Orleans, but it started out as a humble and definitely unromantic digestive aid for the seventeenth-century French diplomat César du Plessis-Praslin. Advised by his doctors that sugar-coated almonds would prevent heartburn (a prescription having no basis in modern medical science), Plessis-Praslin not only ate huge quantities himself but also served huge quantities to his dinner guests. In time, the praline, named for the dyspeptic diplomat but referring to *any* sugar-glazed nut, became a fixture at French tables.

Transported to New Orleans, the praline acquired a more glamorous character as a multi-ingredient candy, usually featuring locally grown pecans, but often some other native variety of nut. The glorified pralines became so popular in eighteenth- and nineteenth-century New Orleans that they were sold on the street by fiercely competing *pralinières,* who displayed their wares on eye-catching salvers.

One particularly exotic praline during this period combined peanuts with popcorn in a sugary frosting. It was called Mais Tac-tac and ultimately evolved into what we call Cracker Jacks. This recipe borrows back the peanut from Mais Tac-tac and uses it to replace the pecan in the "classic" New Orleans praline. Like the classic pecan-based model, Peanut-Buttery Pralines are especially enjoyable served with coffee after a rich and festive meal.

3 cups light brown sugar	*¹/₂ cup peanut butter*
1 cup milk	*2 cups salted dry-roasted peanuts*
¹/₄ teaspoon salt	*2 teaspoons vanilla extract*

1. In heavy, medium saucepan, combine sugar, milk, and salt. Bring to a boil over medium-high heat, stirring frequently.

2. Cover 2–3 minutes until steaming. Uncover and brush down sides of pan with a little water if sugar sticks. Cook, without stirring, until mixture reaches 234–38°F on a candy thermometer (or until a small amount of mixture dropped into cold water forms a soft ball that flattens when removed from water).

3. Remove from heat. Whisk in peanut butter until blended. Cool 1 hour, without stirring.

4. Add peanuts and vanilla. Beat with a wooden spoon until mixture is slightly thickened and smooth.

5. Drop by heaping tablespoonfuls on wax paper coated with vegetable oil cooking spray. Let harden 12 hours. Store candy between sheets of wax paper in airtight container.

PEANUT BUTTER–RUM TRUFFLES

●■▲●■▲●

MAKES 2 DOZEN TRUFFLES

Rich, deeply bittersweet truffles are the crème de la crème of chocolates. Present-day truffles typically have a sleek, domed shape that befits their sophisticated taste. The original truffles, however, always had a somewhat lumpy cocoa coating, making them resemble the earthy truffle mushroom that is such a prized ingredient in French haute cuisine. Indeed, the celebrated chocolates were named after the celebrated fungus—although their respective flavors are worlds apart!

Peanut Butter–Rum Truffles give a refined French twist to the taste of peanut butter. One secret of any good truffle lies in the chilling, and in this particular recipe, the rum flavor develops beautifully in harmony with the peanut butter flavor during the long final period of refrigeration.

¹/₄ cup heavy cream
2 tablespoons dark rum *
¹/₂ teaspoon vanilla extract
¹/₂ cup peanut butter
¹/₄ cup semisweet chocolate chips
3 tablespoons confectioners' sugar

1 tablespoon chilled unsalted butter, quartered
3 tablespoons cocoa powder
¹/₂ cup finely chopped unsalted dry-roasted peanuts

1. In 1-cup measure, combine cream, rum, and vanilla. Set aside.

2. In medium saucepan, combine peanut butter, chips, and sugar over low heat. Stir frequently, until mixture is smooth and thick (about 5 minutes). Whisk in butter, a piece at a time, until melted. Whisk in cream mixture.

3. Refrigerate, stirring occasionally, until mixture is firm enough to mound on spoon (about 2 hours).

4. On foil-lined baking sheet, drop heaping teaspoonfuls of mixture. Shape into balls. Freeze 30 minutes.

5. Place cocoa powder and peanuts on separate pieces of wax paper. Roll each ball first in cocoa, then in peanuts, to cover. Place in paper

---

* If desired, any liqueur may be used instead of rum.

candy cups. Refrigerate between sheets of wax paper in airtight container for up to 2 weeks.

PEANUT BUTTER MOUSSE
IN PHYLLO CUPS
●■▲●■▲●
SERVES 4

Peanut butter is no longer looked upon as a prohibitively high-calorie food. In fact, it's so versatile, tasty, and nutritious—even in small amounts—that health and beauty spas are now using it to add flavor and texture to the dishes they serve.

This dessert is adapted from a peanut butter mousse served at the Canyon Ranch Spa in Tucson, Arizona. As far as grams of fat in peanut butter go, it contains a respectably low 7.3 grams of *monounsaturated* fat per serving, and yet it is mouth-watering—not to mention elegant and visually spectacular. The phyllo (pastry) cups resemble flower petals, adding substance and drama to the dish.

1 cup nonfat ricotta
¼ cup peanut butter
2 tablespoons sugar
2 tablespoons skim milk
1 teaspoon ground cinnamon

1 teaspoon vanilla extract
2 sheets phyllo dough, thawed if frozen
1 cup pureed strawberries (optional)

1. Preheat oven to 375°F. Coat 4 ½-cup ramekins with vegetable oil cooking spray. Set aside.

2. In food processor fitted with a steel blade, process first 6 ingredients until smooth. Spoon into small bowl. Refrigerate, covered, 2 hours.

3. To prepare phyllo cups, place 1 sheet phyllo on counter. Spray entire sheet with vegetable oil cooking spray. Lay remaining sheet on top. Spray again. Cut both sheets in half lengthwise, then cut each half crosswise into 4 (4×6-inch) rectangles, producing a total of 8 (4×6-inch) rectangles, each rectangle with 2 sheets phyllo. Overlap 2 rectangles into each prepared ramekin, gently pushing into center and side to

form cup. Phyllo will extend over top of ramekins. Spray phyllo ends with vegetable oil cooking spray to prevent burning.

4. Place ramekins on baking sheet; bake 7–10 minutes until golden brown. Cool on wire rack. Leave in ramekins until ready to serve. May be made up to 6 hours ahead.

5. Gently lift phyllo cups from ramekins. Place each on medium-size serving plate. Fill each with about ⅓ cup mousse. Spoon pureed strawberries, if desired, around rim of dish.

Bibliography

Anderson, Jean. *The Grass Roots Cookbook*. New York: Times Books, 1977.

Baggett, Nancy. *The International Cookie Cookbook*. New York: Stewart, Tabori & Chang, 1988.

Belk, Sarah. *Around the Southern Table*. New York: Simon & Schuster, 1991.

Berolzheimer, Ruth. *Culinary Arts Institute Encyclopedic Cookbook*. Chicago: Culinary Arts Institute, 1969.

Betty Crocker's Cookbook. New York: Golden Press, 1988.

Bhumichitr, Vatcharin. *Thai Vegetarian Cooking*. New York: Clarkson Potter Publishers, 1991.

Child, Julia. *The Way to Cook*. New York: Alfred A. Knopf, 1989.

Claiborne, Craig. *Craig Claiborne's The New York Times Food Encyclopedia*. New York: Times Books, 1985.

Cunningham, Marion. *The Fannie Farmer Cookbook*. New York: Alfred A. Knopf, 1990.

DeProft, Melanie, ed. *The Culinary Arts American Family Cookbook*. New York: Simon & Schuster, 1971.

Fabricant, Florence. *New Home Cooking*. New York: Clarkson Potter Publishers, 1991.

Fitzgibbon, Theodora. *The Food of the Western World*. New York: Times Books, 1976.

Gethers, Judy. *The Sandwich Book*. New York: Random House, 1990.

Hays, Wilma, and Vernon R. *Foods the Indians Gave Us*. New York: Ives Washburn, Inc., 1973.

Herbst, Sharon Tyler. *Food Lover's Companion*. New York: Barron's, 1990.

Hultman, Tami, ed. *The African News Cookbook*. New York: Penguin Books, 1986.

King, Shirley. *Fish: The Basics*. New York: Simon & Schuster, 1990.

Leahy, Linda Romanelli. *The Oat Bran Cookbook*. New York: Ballantine, 1989.

Leahy, Linda Romanelli. *The All-Natural Sugar-Free Dessert Cookbook*. New York: Dell, 1992.

London, Anne, and Bishov, Bertha Kahn, eds. *The Complete American-Jewish Cookbook*. New York: Harper & Row, 1971.

Mandel, Abby. *Abby Mandel's Cuisinart Classroom*. New York: Harper & Row, 1980.

Mariani, John F. *The Dictionary of American Food and Drink*. New York: Ticknor & Fields, 1983.

Mayer, Paul. *Souffle and Quiche*. Concord, CA: Nitty Gritty Productions, 1972.

McCune, Kelly. *Grill Book*. New York: Harper & Row, 1989.

McGee, Harold. *On Food and Cooking*. New York: Charles Scribner's Sons, 1984.

McNair, James. *Breakfast*. New York: Arbor House, 1987.

Ogden, Bradley. *Breakfast, Lunch and Dinner*. New York: Random House, 1991.

Passimore, Jacki. *The Encyclopedia of Asian Food and Cooking*. New York: Hearst Books, 1991.

Riely, Elizabeth. *The Chef's Companion*. New York: Van Nostrand Reinhold Company, 1986.

Rombauer, Irma S., and Becker, Marion Rombauer. *Joy of Cooking*. New York: Bobbs-Merrill Company, Inc., 1931.

Scicolone, Michele. *The Antipasto Table*. New York: William Morrow, Inc., 1991.

Simon, Andre L., and Howe, Robin. *Dictionary of Gastronomy*. New York: McGraw-Hill, 1970.

Tang, Tommy. *Tommy Tang's Modern Thai Cuisine*. New York: Doubleday, 1991.

Ward, Artemus. *The Encyclopedia of Food*. New York: Peter Smith, 1941.

Weiner, Leslie, and Albright, Barbara. *Simply Scones*. New York: Macmillan Publishing Company, 1988.

Williams, Sallie Y. *The Complete Book of Sauces*. New York: Macmillan Publishing Company, 1990.

The Williamsburg Cookbook. New York: Holt, Rinehart and Winston, 1975.

Zenker, John J., and Zenker, Hazel G. *Cookie Cookery*. New York: M. Evans and Company, Inc., 1969.

Zisman, Larry, and Zisman, Honey. *The Great American Peanut Butter Book*. New York: St. Martin's Press, 1985.

Index

About the Authors

LINDA ROMANELLI LEAHY is a professional recipe developer, teacher, and frequent contributor to food magazines. Former test kitchen director for *Weight Watchers' Magazine,* she has been honored with a Chef des Cuisines Award and a Mac Roberts Award for Culinary Excellence. She is the author of *The Oat Bran Cookbook* (Ballantine, 1989) and *The All-Natural, Sugar-Free Dessert Cookbook* (Dell, 1992). She lives in the Park Slope section of Brooklyn with her husband, Rob.

JACK MAGUIRE is a writer specializing in the fields of home living, self-development, and popular culture. Among his books are *Care and Feeding of the Brain* (Doubleday, 1990) and *What Does Childhood Taste Like?* (Morrow, 1986). He lives in Highland, New York.